THIS PRESENT WORLD

KALOS

The word *kalos* (καλός) means beautiful. It is the call of the good; that which arouses interest, desire: "I am here." Beauty brings the appetite to rest at the same time as it wakens the mind from its daily slumber, calling us to look afresh at that which is before our very eyes. It makes virgins of us all, and of everything—there, before us, lies something that we never noticed before. Beauty consists in *integritas sive perfectio* (integrity and perfection) and *claritas* (brightness/clarity). It is the reason why we rise and why we sleep—that great night of dependence, one that reveals the borrowed existence of all things, if, that is, there is to be a thing at all, or if there is to be a person at all. Here lies the ground of all science, of philosophy, and of all theology, indeed, of our each and every day.

This series will seek to provide intelligent-yet-accessible volumes that have the innocence of beauty and of true adventure, and in so doing remind us all again of that which we took for granted, most of all thought itself.

SERIES EDITORS:
Conor Cunningham, Eric Austin Lee, and Joseph Terry

This Present World

APHORISMS FOR KNOWING GOD

. . .

Steven DeLay

CASCADE *Books* · Eugene, Oregon

THIS PRESENT WORLD
Aphorisms for Knowing God

Copyright © 2025 Steven DeLay. All rights reserved. Except for brief quotations in critical publications or reviews, no part of this book may be reproduced in any manner without prior written permission from the publisher. Write: Permissions, Wipf and Stock Publishers, 199 W. 8th Ave., Suite 3, Eugene, OR 97401.

Cascade Books
An Imprint of Wipf and Stock Publishers
199 W. 8th Ave., Suite 3
Eugene, OR 97401

www.wipfandstock.com

PAPERBACK ISBN: 979-8-3852-4707-3
HARDCOVER ISBN: 979-8-3852-4708-0
EBOOK ISBN: 979-8-3852-4709-7

Cataloguing-in-Publication data:

Names: DeLay, Steven, 1986– [author].

Title: This present world : aphorisms for knowing God / Steven DeLay.

Description: Eugene, OR: Cascade Books, 2025 | Series: Kalos | Includes index.

Identifiers: ISBN 979-8-3852-4707-3 (paperback) | ISBN 979-8-3852-4708-0 (hardcover) | ISBN 979-8-3852-4709-7 (ebook)

Subjects: LCSH: Aphorisms and apothegms. | Philosophy and religion. | Aphorisms and proverbs. | Phenomenology.

Classification: BL51 D45 2025 (paperback) | BL51 (ebook)

VERSION NUMBER 071125

As always,

For Gabriella

Now we have received, not the spirit of the world, but the spirit which is of God; that we might know the things that are freely given to us of God.

— 1 CORINTHIANS 2:12

Contents

Preface | ix

Aphorisms | 1

Index of Names | 115

Preface

IT WOULD BE AS presumptuous as it would be futile for an author to attempt to thoroughly justify his work with an initial word about it. In the end, a work, and especially so a philosophical one, proves to accomplish its stated aim, in part, depending on whether or not its readers judge it to have spoken for itself. Still, it seems fitting to at least state at the outset how the present work aims to contribute to the phenomenological task of illuminating our human condition before God. This seems all the more imperative when, as here, the form of the work itself, which consists in a series of aphorisms, is liable to obscure what that aim even is. A brief comment, then, on the nature of phenomenological philosophy is in order.

As someone who years ago was drawn to the traditions of phenomenology and existentialism, I remain convinced that philosophy's ultimate question is the meaning of human existence. Having now written a number of books that have all in their own ways attempted to respond to that question, I also remain convinced that writing philosophy can contribute to crystallizing life's meaning—attempting to articulate what we take to be the meaning of life enriches and deepens life itself. Not everyone has to write, of course. Nor does everyone have to engage in philosophy. And, to be sure, there are plenty of other questions besides the meaning of existence that are philosophical. Nonetheless, the meaning of existence is *the* philosophical question, it seems to me, which is why, in the course of writing on that question in prior books, I have found myself relying on the phenomenological tradition to do so. For me, it has been those associated with the "theological turn" in phenomenology—in particular, Michel Henry, Jean-Louis Chrétien, Jean-Luc Marion, and Jean-Yves Lacoste—who have provided the philosophical horizon in which my own thought has been able to orient and establish itself.

Preface

With an eye to elucidating human existence, phenomenology is always on the hunt for experiential truths. And because it must measure itself against experience, it seems to me inevitable that for this reason it is also an existential philosophy. What sometimes in the Anglophone world is called "existential phenomenology," then, is nearly tautological, for a phenomenology that did not think existence would not *be* phenomenological. So far, so good—nothing about this understanding of phenomenological philosophy would strike anyone as anything but banal. For my own part, however, I have found it impossible to ruminate on the meaning of human existence apart from thinking of God. And so, from the beginning, it has always seemed plain to me that phenomenology should, indeed must, consider the question of God. For if human life must be lived before God, so too must the philosophical attempt to reflect on that life. A phenomenology that faces squarely our being-before-God is thus a Christian existentialism. Others, of course, will disagree, there being some having gone so far as to contend that phenomenology must, to the contrary, bracket God from its purview. I have elsewhere tried my best to offer various arguments in favor of my own conception of phenomenological philosophy—its method and matter.

This book is different in that regard. A book of aphorisms such as this one inevitably is fragmentary. It may for that reason be thought to be unsystematic. But I doubt any philosophical system can do full justice to life anyway, so, in a way, methodologically speaking, at least, aphoristic reflections on life, which admittedly remain impressional, provisional, and circumstantial, come closest to conforming to the essence of the very things they aim to express. In professing to see what I see, I am fully cognizant that there will be others who will be unconvinced. But these aphorisms express what I believe I have seen, and it bears emphasizing that those who believe that I am "only seeing things" must ultimately appeal to nothing more than what they believe themselves to see. This means, I think, that there is no final court of appeal, at least in this life, to determine who is right. Some may see this as a sign that something somewhere has gone wrong, that what is being brought forward is no longer, strictly speaking, philosophical. I prefer to think that intractable disagreement is here the inevitable consequence of trying to live up to the phenomenological task of saying something about the meaning of existence, so far as that meaning is revealed to us.

Those who deserve to be thanked for making this book possible are too numerous to be named. I trust that in reading the pages to follow, they

Preface

will recognize the mark they have made on me and thus, in turn, on the work too.

San Luis Obispo, California
December 2024

1

In the end

Every word is a response to the Word.

2

Epiphanic—our first time encountering God

In the first proof for God's existence in his Third Meditation, Descartes in effect notes that to have the idea of God is *ipso facto* to know there is a God, as only God would be capable of revealing the idea of himself to us. That this very thought should be dismissed as the mark of a childlike understanding, something at which the learned take themselves justifiably to scoff, only further recommends its truth. "You have hidden these things from the wise and learned, and revealed them to babes." Having grown into adulthood, which really in this respect is a state of blindness, those who deny it admit that they have lost the wisdom of innocence.

3
To endure consolation's wound requires strength

Eventually, someone says to us that God merely is a consolation. (The implication being that God is thus an illusion.) We are young, and initially this apparent insight appears to us to be powerful. Some never recover from it—they live the rest of their lives under the thumb of its presumed authority. True maturity—not the blind variety that is all too common, what by the world is considered maturity—is outgrowing this immaturity's spell, and seeing that there was never anything wrong with consolation, to begin with. How *immature* to pretend that the truth should *not* be consoling! There is no one who believes anything that one does not to some degree find consoling (even the most supposed bitter and ugly of reputed truths have their own sweetness).

4
The cult of false strength, i.e., those who profess to be beyond the need for consolation

Those who criticize belief in God for being a consolation know this better than anyone. To them, acknowledging God would be misery, and so they console themselves with the consoling thought that belief in God is just a consolation.

5
To be free of illusion is to accept that God alone consoles absolutely

What essential connection, then, lies between illusion and consolation? The one who rejects God on the basis that such belief is thought merely to be a consolation, and so an illusion, only testifies against himself. That something is consoling needn't mean it is false. True, a lie can be consoling. But so, too, can the truth. More to the point, the very same truth can be the source of consolation for one, while for another its recognition would be the cause of the most unspeakable agony or despair.

6

The illusion of worldly shrewdness

What worse imaginable illusion is there than to reject a truth for illusion when in the grips of the illusion that it is too consoling to be true? Only a fool, which is to say, only an adult who thinks he knows what mature wisdom involves, could ever have come to be so lost, so enervated, so grotesquely estranged from the simplicity of childhood's wisdom.[1]

7

Anticipating the absurdist

The subject of consolation and God inevitably puts us in mind of Camus. But we will come to him later on the matter of rebellion.

8

Revelation is self-revealing

To say that truth always is a revelation, then, is to say that it reveals who we are just as much as it reveals itself. *The truth reveals*—what? In virtue of whether we welcome it with gladness and find it a reason for consolation, or whether instead we reject it as an illusion, because we hate it, and don't want for it to be true, the truth does not thereby reveal just itself—more, it exposes us for who we are and, above all, reveals our illusions about ourselves to others, sometimes even to us.

---

1. Throughout the work, I use male-pronouns exclusively, even when speaking of humanity generally. I do so not only for grammatical reasons but also because, aesthetically, I find gender-neutral constructions, such as "he or she" and "him or her," less economical and less elegant. It is not intended to be exclusionary in any way.

9
Unbelief is disobedience

The atheists love to make so much of the virtue of honesty—"intellectual honesty," "intellectual clean conscience," etc. etc. (I have just now been thinking of Camus, so here again I think of his notion of "the wild longing for clarity.") But if he were to be honest, the atheist should say that it isn't that he doesn't believe there is a God but rather that he doesn't want there to be one. It is not that he believes God does not exist. He tries to convince himself that this is what he believes by willfully putting God continually out of his mind.

10
The atheist doth protest too much

The atheist must constantly attempt to persuade others of his unbelief because he has never entirely persuaded himself. The same joke that can be said of vegans can thus be said of atheists—"How do you know someone is an atheist? Don't worry; he will tell you."

11
Being oneself is being before God, even if that means standing alone

A faith that stood wholly alone even were it the last vestige of faith left remaining on the earth—that is conceivable. But an atheism? No, never. What deeper proof could there be that atheism at heart is for the herd? Or said otherwise: in this world, faith is the true iconoclasm.

12

We are only satisfied by living by every word that proceeds from the mouth of God

It is true that the gospel seeks to convert all men everywhere into becoming its disciples. And yet (and this is absolutely essential to it), one alone can follow it, even were one the last and only one on earth to do so. Its universal aspirations for all men spring forth from the recognition of its truth being one able to withstand complete solitude. With atheism, it is the reverse. It perpetually appeals to the notions of independence, autonomy, and so forth. But then it measures its own success by numbers—by how many converts it has attained. For the atheist, truth is a matter of *progress*, which here really amounts to little more than converting others to join its cause. For all of its disdain for Christian evangelization, it sells a belief that by its own admission must feast on new flesh, rather than the meagerness of whatever sustenance it purports to carry within itself.

13

Take a breath

We write for the same reason that we think—once we've begun, there's no end in sight.

14

If Plato had read the Old Testament

Plato said that thinking is the soul speaking with itself. This is superior to only letting others speak within oneself, which is to go through life thoughtlessly. But still better to have silenced everyone, including oneself, so that the soul only hears God. Beyond thinking, and speaking, there must be listening. That is its own form of thoughtlessness—the highest one imaginable, known only to faith.

15
Things, not names

It is an extraordinarily difficult thing to think any thought of importance or to follow a chain of reasoning without immediately being tempted to identify it with some figure of thought—a great name, a Plato, Aristotle, Kant, or whomever it may be. We always desire to situate our thoughts in a collective space, a conversation. To have a thought, and to be comfortable having it without in turn assigning it to someone else—only then is thinking poised to contemplate what lies beyond thought.

16
The first time encountering God (cont'd)

Forget, then, what Descartes says about the idea of God. Had one never discovered that Descartes had thought it as well, would it for that reason have been any less revealing? The truth resides in the fact of what was revealed—not that someone else has thought to say it too.

17

Fragments

Thought can be systematic without our having the whole in sight from the beginning. We must at the very least believe this to be so, otherwise we would never bother to begin writing. And even if the notion that a written work can be systematic despite its author not having its totality in view from the work's inception may be a consoling thought, and for that reason one we might view with suspicion, it is an inescapable one. Call this dimension to any act of sustained writing a "practical postulate" of the art, if you like. This is the difference between thinking and writing—the latter testifies that there is some end, some sense of the whole, to which it is pointing, even if it makes no claim to be able to ever reach it. How could we write unless we had already some sense of what we felt we had to say prior to knowing what that precisely is? All writing is in that respect fragmentary—it collects, piece by piece, thought's crumbs into something that holds more or less together once it has been stitched to paper. (No written work is ever completed. There is always more to say, or what could have been said, or could have been said differently. One must simply decide when to consider it finished. That is what systematicity is—knowing how to judge when what's been left off the page can rightly stay there.)

18

The philosopher's isolation

Philosophy's desire for systematicity, as epitomized most extravagantly in the philosophy of nineteenth-century German idealism, ultimately stems from the yearning to be understood and to be able to see that others have come to understand us, or at least acknowledge that we have a claim to have that yearning for understanding recognized. That is the inner tension of the philosophical life. Philosophy begins when we, unlike the majority of those around us, are sufficiently dissatisfied with leaving things unquestioned, so we in turn at last choose to think, and then write, what we have thought. We write, thus, in order to justify this decision to have indulged the impulse to alleviate our original dissatisfaction. And yet, the very ones whom we would like most to justify ourselves before—those who themselves see no need for the philosophical life—are precisely the ones with whom we cannot communicate. They will never read us! Our readers, instead, are those themselves who have also felt called to write—but do *they* need what we say? If they are anything like us, they no more need our words than we need theirs. Philosophers, it would seem, are like lone wolves, forever roving the barren woods looking to join a pack. Solitude, solitude, solitude—always this hungry solitude.

19

May all be one in Christ

It follows, as it were, that the philosophical life, so construed, cannot be the ultimate aim of life. The good life—the *best*, the *highest*, the *most noble*, the *truest*, call it what you will—must at once respect man's simultaneous needs for solitude and connection. It cannot be thought, or writing out our thoughts, that brings about this desired unity in singularity. Only the life that is hidden in Christ can.

20

Real philosophy leads us back to the reality of life

That the philosophical life's inability to accomplish its own aim points to something lying beyond itself that would accomplish its own aim is precisely why the "second naïveté" of which Paul Ricœur spoke is possible. If we make the "leap," we return to the ordinary, transfigured. (Forgive the fact that we should put the point by reference to Ricœur and with an allusion to Kierkegaard. Old habits die hard.)

21

Truth is no one's possession

An objection: this is all presumption. Who are *you* to tell us such things? Or, put differently: "You're no Paul Ricœur!" you will say. But that is no criticism—who else could I be but me? And if I told you something that I once thought for myself is what Descartes himself had thought also, does that not show that my own thought (and Descartes's thought as well) is worth considering? But again, always this name-dropping. To let a thought stand truly on its own two feet—that is intellectual faith, that is wisdom, or at least the seeds of it.

22

See for yourself what is there to be seen, not what others say they see

"You must become like a child"—think like a child, think for oneself, in the pure reverie of joyful freedom. That is the wisdom of God. Not an egoism that has so crowded out any space so as to exclude accommodating anything besides itself, but rather a solipsism, if you like, that ignores what others might think or say about what it thinks, so that, when all else has been muted, the wonder and mystery of creation can finally speak again through that silence. This is why no less an authority than St. Paul says that those who profess themselves to be wise, but are not, fail to see God through creation. They are too preoccupied with what they call thinking, which for them is solely a matter restricted to worrying over the opinions and possible objections of others.

23

See for yourself what is there to be seen, not what others say they see (cont'd)

Even if we think it a contradiction to quote St. Paul right after having extolled the virtue of not clothing the legitimacy of one's own thoughts in the garb of another's reputation, here the crucial fact remains that St. Paul tells us to direct ourselves to what is seen. The authority is not so much in his words alone, but in the authority of that to which his words remind us to subject ourselves. "What do *you* see, if you should be so bold as to choose to see as a child again?" That is the measure.

24

Rigor in philosophy is knowing a work writes itself

Is it still a work of thought, that is to say, a systematic work, a philosophical work, if the work's author worries, in the midst of writing it, whether he has much left to say? Or worries whether he has still too much to say? No work would be written if every word were only committed to the page with clear and distinct certainty over what remained to be said, much less over how to say it. In a way, a book writes itself. The author merely dictates what comes to mind. And what author can say he is the author of his own thoughts?

25

A crumb from Jean-Louis Chrétien's table

The Latin *inspirare* means "to breathe into" or "to blow into." (That is something I learned from Chrétien, I confess.) This is what inspiration is—letting pass through us what has arisen from elsewhere. A thought, a word, anything truly worth saying—always, it is a revelation.

26

In the end (cont'd)

How else could a thought or word be shared, or better, be worth sharing, unless it never had been ours to start with? That is how the Word speaks—so intimately within us that there is no doubt it is destined for us, but always from an elsewhere so distant from ourselves that we are sure that in sharing it we share something worthwhile—not ourselves, but Christ in us.

27

Reader #2

"What is this? All of sudden he's talking of Christ? But how? I see no argument! No transition! Nothing—it's almost as if it were—yes, a leap!" If that is how it must be, how else can one proceed but by it? There will be no outward justification for it having taken place, nor any manual or formula for how you might do so along with me—only the attestation that it has occurred here in me.

28

Carry me

Don't fear, don't worry. If the inspiration leaves, it will come again. It has left and returned before, and it will again. That is faith.

29

People are not books

Is it really true that you never can judge a book by its cover? With a book, perhaps not. But with people? You can judge others quite perceptively on first impression.

30

A question for myself

I, one, we—so many names in which one (or better, *I, we*?) can and does commonly speak. Suppose philosophy, in part, comes down to the articulation of a claim to essential truth about reality—how else could such claims be responsibly advanced but by anyone other than by oneself, which is to say, in the name of *I myself* or *me*? Whence, then, this plurality of voices—this *we*, for example? Or, what of this anonymity hovering over the page, lurking always in the recesses of one's thoughts—this *one*?

31

I must decrease

The only way to clarify for oneself—*myself*—the place from which we—or better, *I*—speak, is to understand how one's thought has come to occupy the place it has currently. All thought, however, is rooted in the life of the thinker. In order to make sense of all these perspectives of one's own thought, of these thoughts about life, and about God, it is necessary to go back to the source of it all, in short, the beginning of one's very own life (or at least the first memories that we have of it). All thought ultimately stems from childhood, from the impressions we have formed, the choices we have made, the paths we ultimately have chosen to take, for better or for worse. If thought always remains inexhaustible, it is because its origin contains within itself the trace of its encounter with what no thought could ever have given itself—Infinity, as the philosophers call it, which is really to say, the Word.

32

A good man out of the treasure of his heart brings forth what is good

When you feel that you are in danger of losing your way, listen to your heart. Those who think they know their Bible will tell you that such a phrase—"listen to your heart"—is nowhere found in the Scriptures. Typically, such an observation is made with the idea in mind that listening to your heart would entail indulging your desires, your whims, your lusts—in short, *not* listening to God. But that is not what it means to listen to your heart in the sense worthy of being recommended. Listen to God—yes, above all, always listen to God! But how else will one so listen but in the heart? That is what the Scriptures mean by the "inner man." Sometimes this interior space where God speaks is expressed in terms of man's having a conscience. So, no matter what others say, whether it be worldly others who have not read the Bible and don't have the slightest concern themselves for God (and so who think listening to your heart would be silly if that were taken to mean listening to God), or else serious religious types who claim to know the misguidedness of listening to your heart (because they think it means suggesting doing something other than God's will), ignore them—ignore them all, and still listen to your heart. To listen to the heart—there is no other way to know what God demands of us.

33

The heart listens

Not to listen to what God tells us in our heart is to lose our way, no matter how otherwise attractive or alluring or justifiable we at the time tell ourselves the alternative path we take instead may be. Henceforth, life becomes little more than correcting for an error—yet we never truly get around to righting it. The errors steadily compound, and before we know it, we have strayed so far that we are so lost that we scarcely remember who we were. There are people who have never listened to their hearts, or at least ceased listening long ago, such that their whole entire lives end up having been one big error. Never having lived the life they should, it was as if they never lived at all. "Depart from me, for I never knew you."

34

Taste of evil

More so than even the death of someone we know, our first and deepest experience of death, because it is the first blow to our innocence, is the discovery in childhood that our friend we so love has chosen to lose heart—that he has chosen to change, by choosing to go wrong. For a time after that decision, he hovers in a state of indecision—nothing has yet been fully decided. He has strayed, of course, but he knows that he has. *He still recognizes it as a fall.* There thus remains hope that he may return, may seek restoration, may hope to become again the one he had been before having lost his way. And then—the worst happens. Death, spiritual death, comes. It is not just that he chooses to plunge deeper into darkness—now he even comes to resent you for it, because you are a reminder of the innocence he wants to forget, that he wants to believe was mere naivety. *This* is our first taste of death—the death of the friend who becomes the stranger.

35

408

To come to need to believe that purity of heart, that innocence, had only been reserved for the child who had not known any better—that "growing up" is somehow realizing the inevitability of having to come around to accepting that such innocence will for the rest of life be but a memory until it is one day no longer even that—what a fall! Yes, what a terrific fall, this lapsarian condition that far too many view as a mere matter of course. They assume, evidently, that the stages on life's way should lead to perdition.

36

Chameleon

Do others think often of the past, of those they knew from many years ago? So often we are told not to live in the past, to move on, to get on with it, to focus on the present, to look to the future. All this hustle and bustle amid each of our daily lives wherever we happen to now find ourselves, all this pretending that we all have come from nowhere, as if we do not all carry with us the weight of our pasts. Only the world could treat such inhuman callousness with indifference. Even worse, this forgetting is actually encouraged, is presented as somehow noble (*mature*: there's that word again)—it would be too nostalgic, we hear it said, to concern oneself with what those we once knew were like before they went on to become what they are now, to wonder why they have become as they are, to wonder how they understand, if they understand at all, how the past they shared with us has put them on the path leading to where they are presently. If having such thoughts is said to be overly nostalgic, is not it worse never to have such thoughts at all? What could be less human, more selfish, than to live in willful forgetfulness of what once was, as though it never mattered?

37

Douceur

A sweet nostalgia that sees the exigency of the present in light of the dignity of the past—only that ensures we remain tender at heart, ready for what may come, receptive so that we might enjoy the future's bounty with gratitude.

38

The dignity of what was

If we do not maintain a reverence for the beauty of what once mattered, even long ago, nothing we take to matter currently in the present will either. We will have become too shallow for anything to touch us or to stay with us—in time, we will only look on what we think matters today with the same cold indifference as we look now on yesterday.

39

Homesickness

To lose an appreciation for the past is to lose the yearning for eternity.

40

False positivity

We sometimes shrink from reliving the past in memory, because we do not want to bear the ache. Better, so we think, to put it out of mind. What a danger, however, to make this shying away from the past a habit! For time cannot be fooled any better than we can fool ourselves. All it does is harden the heart. And so, in time, it is true perhaps that whoever does so no longer feels the pains locked away in the chest of time that he has chosen not to open—the embarrassments, the mistakes, the regrets, the happinesses you no longer know, all the things you once liked about yourself that are no longer true of yourself, all the things you liked of those you once knew that are no longer true of them. All this, to be sure, is avoided. Yet how great the cost! You may no longer have to experience the stings of the past, yet you have now inured yourself to the present also.

41

An open heart

Don't be bereft of tenderness for the past, lest you be dead to all else too. Don't forget the past, lest you forget who you are, till you are nobody at all. These sorts of truisms—even if they are just that—must never be forgotten, no matter how irritating others who reject them find them to be.

42

Carry me (cont'd)

It is easy enough to write about how confidence in inspiration is a trust well-placed. Far harder to write with such actual inspiration itself.

43

The light of innocence

We must ourselves live in such a way that protecting a child's joy and innocence isn't felt to be an exercise in merely humoring or indulging a stage the child will inevitably outgrow. We must in our own lives be such that this goodness has the promise of a viable future—a way to go, an example to follow, a light that has shown the Light from which it has itself been illuminated from within. Not the world's light, but the Lord's.

44

What calls for speech

If there were no ineffable, we would not write.

45

The ineffable doesn't render writing otiose or contradictory

Contrary to what this may initially appear to entail, ineffability doesn't make writing a fool's errand. Anything we succeed in saying truly by words directs others back to the silence from which such truth was first communicated to us. Reading, too, for this same reason, takes root in these great fields of silence in which everyone's thoughts are sown. That is why reading profound writing can be so instructive—it reveals within us what we had already known was there but forgotten, or what we didn't want to hear because we have gone astray, and thus of what we needed most to be reminded.

46

Receiving blessings

Too much time is squandered pining for future blessings. Unless we are already grateful, would we even be present to enjoy them, were they to arrive? Recognize that life itself is a gift, and we feel immediately that life itself is sufficient unto itself. This is what Job learned, and each of us can learn it also.

47

All life is aquatic

Jean-Louis Chrétien, Paul Claudel, and Marilynne Robinson all meditate intently on the nature of water. For Claudel, water is what quenches our thirst because we are liquid creatures. That is to say, not just beings recurringly in need of water for the continuation of this life, but also beings for whom our eternal, heavenly destination will itself be aquatic. ("And God made the firmament, and divided the waters which were under the firmament from *the waters which were above the firmament:* and it was so" [Gen 1:7]; italics added). And for Chrétien, like Claudel also, water is sacramental, as the communicative medium of baptism. It is Robinson who considers these two reflections of water most thoroughly. Water, she says, is both elemental and spiritual, belonging to this world's heavenly realms in the sky, and yet also indicating a kingdom of still even higher waters. Claudel, Chrétien, and Robinson perceive that water is a tangible symbol for the Holy Spirit—fluid, cleansing, purifying, refreshing. It is not that we *associate* water with the Spirit, but that the Spirit communicates to us through it.

48

Droplets

"Hurry! Get inside!" No, the next time it rains, even if it is downpouring, rather than staying inside or taking an umbrella to stay dry, go out in it. Get wet. Let the droplets fall as the sparrow does, which is to say, let them fall wherever and however they may, with no obstruction, but rather only as the Father wills. Surrender to the dousing. Remember what it was to be a child who had loved the rain, and understand that it is a grace to again experience not fleeing it but instead enjoying being wet. Then you will feel how the rain descends from on High, elemental and excessive, not from this world's heavenly clouds but from the Kingdom of Heaven, whose emissaries consist not only of the invisible angels but of each and every single one of these precious little visible droplets.

49

What is metaphor anyway?

Why should these thoughts of water be judged peculiar, extravagant, or, as so often is said of what in fact are the most primal truths, *metaphorical*? That everything is liquid inasmuch as all things consist in the Spirit of Christ—what could be more concrete? Even the very air we breathe is itself nothing but veiled water, as any muggy summer night stickily impresses. We fail to glean the Spirit's pervasiveness, only because we are like fish who don't know they're in water.

50

The trees always say something

Thomas Merton once wrote that "trees saying nothing," to describe periods of spiritual dryness. Yet it is not quite true that they ever go wholly silent. Notice how they grow skyward, stretching their arms to the Father of Lights. When we feel earth-ridden, dry as forsaken soil, our eye can always follow the tree's ascent, and see in it a reminder of our own vocation to do the same.

51

Refinement

It is only when some terrible affliction has rendered us forlorn that we realize we were never truly alone. God was always already there, though we had failed to notice. Even our greatest sufferings, betrayal, bereavement, or persecution, rather than serving as cause for bitterness, can be an occasion for gratitude, for when we are alone with nobody else but God, when everyone else has abandoned us but him, we realize that we had not been sufficiently grateful for what is the sweetest gift of all—his steadfastness.

52

What Nicodemus sought

To only be able to recollect our childhood with fondness once we have made peace with God is certainly a step in the right direction, far better than having to disavow the past entirely out of the ongoing shame of an adulthood in which we had remained lost from God. Nonetheless, this mere recollection presupposes the perpetuation of a fall. We have changed, otherwise it would not be necessary to strive to become as we once were. Innocence can become a kind of second nature, by effort, but it is still never totally pristine, because it must never forget that everything has become a project of restoration after having chosen to demolish what should have never been brought to ruins. God will build us up, and we must never cease thanking him for not having left us to our own ashes.

53

Empathy

Someone will say that such thoughts of isolation and solitude are too self-directed and solipsistic. The claim will be: experiencing such isolation is really only that, a *feeling*, for in fact we are always already with others. Fair enough—but how will you ever counsel the other in his time of isolation, in his time of forsakenness, if you have never faced the trial for yourself? We must endure our own periods of darkness so that later we can honestly tell others during theirs that there is hope, that such seasons fade.

54
Remember God's mercy

We choose to fall, to taste evil. The Garden is not only a historic and cosmic state of creation that obtained once, never to be repeated. The fall occurs again and again in the heart of each man who exiles himself from God by following the example of Adam.

55
Pride's tentacles

So, you have fallen? What then? The choice not immediately to stand back up is as much a choice as was the original one to have debased oneself. What else perpetuates sin, the rejection of God's grace, but a prideful self-pity that perseveres in the notion that its own misery is a sweetness it cannot bear to live without? Alienation from God is rooted in the intoxication of presumption—of believing that we can always get around to repenting later, that *we* will be the thief on the cross.

56
Prince Myskin the cat

Hamann thought that the animals speak, but we simply lack the ears to comprehend their language. Wittgenstein thought that if a lion could speak, we in any case would not understand it, for our respective forms of life are incommensurable. In the world to come, however, there will only be one form of life ("Christ *is* all and in all"), for everything will have become what it was always called to be. Not only will the lion lie with the lamb, but we shall all at last talk to one another as brotherly creatures.

57
Nature's canticle

A symposium of creatures praising the Creator—that is one suitable, however inadequate, image for the new heavens and the new earth.

58

The source of all love is God

To love the beloved so absolutely that intolerable is the very thought of living life without her were she to die first, that is a great selfless love. To love so devotedly that to die before the beloved will be a hope fulfilled—again, that is a great selfless love. And yet, it is still tinged with an inescapable self-interestedness, because everything comes back to a matter of what the lover desires in light of what he cannot bear. Even the most selfless, even sacrificial, of merely human loves that would lead one to die, cannot have the slightest thing to do with the order of redemption. There is a deep theological truth to this statement, of course.

59

The simplicity of Christ

Dostoevsky wrote famously in a letter, "If someone proved to me that Christ is outside the truth and that in reality the truth were outside of Christ, then I should prefer to remain with Christ rather than with the truth." That is correct, and it is a truth whose significance should in no way be diminished. But what a joy it is to see that Christ's beauty is worthy of such devotion, and then furthermore to know that he rewards this reverence by indeed being the truth. What joy that we needn't worship an image of the Ideal but can conform ourselves to its image by following its Person. If we could live every moment of our lives fully in this blessed knowledge, we would be ecstatic.

60

The illogicality of "dark" logic

Kierkegaard's definition of despair, according to which all of despair's myriad forms essentially are a matter of one's refusing to be who one is, which is to say, who God is calling one to become, is entirely correct. However, that one should choose to be in despair is a mystery that never admits of an answer (at least not in this life)—"pride," "spite," "envy." No matter what explanation the choice to be in despair is given, we feel that we haven't yet grasped fully the *why*. "You live in despair because you are proud"—yes, but *why* is one proud? "You live in despair because you have chosen to be spiteful"—yes, but *why* the choice to be so? And so on. Despair, then, like all evil, is without ground—it is without reason. That is ultimately why those who succumb to it are without excuse.

61

Answering Feuerbach

Feuerbach contends that the God of theology, modern theology particularly so, is a distorted excogitation of childlike religious experience. He does not dismiss the childlike encounter itself with the divine as something illusory. What he criticizes is theology's decision to posit the existence of a transcendent God on the basis of that original religious experience. Feuerbach is partly right, though at the same time he is also importantly wrong. He is right inasmuch as the rationalistic theology of his day should not be taken seriously, for the God it *conceives* is just that—a *concept*, which is to say, an *idol* of the true and living God. However, this is where Feuerbach took a wrong turn—he denies the existence of the Christian God in the name of a childlike belief he praises but which, in fact, is not sufficiently childlike. The God of reason is a theoretical posit that has no bearing on experience, to be sure, yet the God of revelation is unveiled in the depths of the very religious experience Feuerbach himself claims to champion over theology. Feuerbach's trouble, like all other atheists, is that he never fully became as a child, and so he failed to discern Christ in innocence.

62

Sympathy for the devil

The phrase "sympathy for the devil" doesn't explicitly appear anywhere in the Scriptures. Anyone who loves God is bound to notice it everywhere in daily life, however. For example, those who hate God but would never say so openly have more sympathy for a righteous man's persecutors than for the good man who suffers it. Persecution, thus, is demonstration enough that there are indeed those who have sympathy for the devil, for were it not the case, there would be no persecution. Persecution is possible only because it is tolerated by those who pretend not themselves to be actively engaged in it. Their silence in the face of it is a complicity without which persecution would be impossible. Although they do not confess their sympathy for the devil openly, they might as well, for they bend over backwards to coddle the minions who do serve the prince of darkness. While "sympathy for the devil" is never mentioned in the Bible, the pervasiveness in daily life of what can be termed "sympathy for the persecutors" explains why we should thus find what is said indirectly about the matter in Scripture: "A prophet is not without honor," etc., etc.

63

Nietzsche's revenge?

Nietzsche has received the prize he so deeply coveted now that today he is extolled for his life's work. But he himself never actually affirmed his own life in the fashion his thought suggests we ought. Rather than affirming life on its own terms, instead he sought consolation in the assurance that future generations would recognize his greatness. This yearning for that type of legacy was a form of revenge against those he felt were doing him an injustice. A concern for posterity is among the surest signs of a resentful spirit. A far higher ideal free of any such resentment is to seek the honor that comes from God only rather than men.

64

What has Nietzsche gained, if he has lost his soul?

This is not quite right—has *Nietzsche* received his prize? His *name* is honored among men, of course, but as for the man himself, we must shudder. The *name* remains among us. But where is *he*?

65

Walking thoughts

We know we are growing in grace when the hypocrisy and cruelty of those who hate us no longer embitters us as they wish that it would. Rousseau comes very close to reaching this kind of serenity when in his *Reveries of the Solitary Walker* he describes being indifferent to those who consider themselves his enemy. That kind of indifference is but a first step along the long path to full peace, however. Eventually, we go farther, by praying that those who hate us may find that peace of God too.

66

The world is upside down

How strange that almost everyone will obey worldly authority with such unqualified zeal, particularly when it is evil men in charge who give the orders. Yet speak of the necessity of submission to God, and these same people who usually are willing to do slavishly as they are told act suddenly as if they have never heard of duty. When in the book of Acts it is said that the early Christians were described as "those who turn the world upside down," that is why, in part. The idea that God must be obeyed, that God is the true authority rather than evil men with their wicked systems, was contrary to everything our inverted world takes for granted. What is up is treated as down, what is down as up. The world is upside down and does not even see it.

67

Vice is slavery

Adulthood is a life of indulging one's preferred vices, and in this lies the promise of freedom, even happiness. If there are any two bigger lies of the present world that do more damage to all our lives, I cannot think what they are.

68

We are what we read

Someone told me he read somewhere, perhaps in Borges, that the whole of our conscious knowledge consists in whatever the last ten books we have read happen to be. This is probably true, which is why the Bible should be read every day.

69

The earnestness of Scripture

When I read the Bible, I look for answers, and I find them. When I read anything else, no matter how beautiful, insightful, gripping, moving, or otherwise remarkable, it is not the same. There is still always a sense of *amusement* when reading anything else, whereas reading the Scriptures is always serious business—or so it should be.

70

Weeding

This fallen world is a field in which evil's weeds sprout continually. There will always be more, but the good man is undeterred and never ceases to pull them up anyway. Weeding out evil—it is not just to cultivate one's own garden but to lend one's own hand to the labor of tending God's.

71
"Occupy till I come"

Note well that when the parable of the wheat and the tares speaks of evil men not being gathered up and discarded until the final judgment, it is the angels, not men, who are told to wait. Till then, it is good men who must be occupied, must be at work, until the Lord comes.

72
Nothing ever happens . . .until . . .

All explanation is ultimately circular. So too is all experience, until the moment when God ruptures the worldliness to which we had come to accustom ourselves. Experiencing this call of God is like being stirred from a deep slumber or a spell of sleep walking. We sit up, rub our eyes, and meet the day, one now suffused with the light of eternity.

73
The Longhouse

The highest thoughts are only as pure as the air in which they are breathed into us. University offices have become too stuffy and polluted for such thinking.

74
"Oh, so it's professional jealousy"

Our enemies initially are driven by jealousy. God's way of rewarding us for our faithfulness is that later their defeat is manifest in the fact that their hatred no longer rages on from jealousy, but from envy.

75

What St. Paul said to young Timothy

No one comes to the Father except through Christ. Moreover, no one knows the Father but those to whom Christ reveals him. And because Christ can only be known through an acceptance of the suffering that comes by following him, we stand to attain the promise of eternal life only when we are not offended by Christ and choose to follow him nonetheless, no matter what hardships or deprivations come from doing so. Whoever comes to understand what is necessary to attain eternal life accordingly learns daily the ineluctability of drinking of the same cup of which Christ did. A salvation without suffering is superstition.

76

Righteous gladness

That all the various pleasures of this world thought to lie in power, fame, or riches pale in comparison to the satisfaction of knowing Christ, even when in suffering and in persecution, is something those who live for the world ridicule. We hear skeptics so often criticize faith as dull and dreary, or inhibiting and stultifying. Faith certainly requires that we break with hedonism, and yet, despite demanding that we elevate ourselves above a life governed by the pursuit of pleasure, those who die to the world end up more content than any hedonist ever does. Suck all the marrow from this world's bones, and we still hunger. But hunger for righteousness instead, and we are filled. How sad that the carnal spend the whole of their lives rejecting the only source of true abiding joy possible in the time that leads to death, only to slave away in pursuit of its counterfeits.

77
What is metaphysics?

One popular definition of metaphysics today is that it is philosophical inquiry that attempts to make sense of things. Yet philosophy inevitably fails to make sense of existence because it dismisses as superstition the truths of Christian revelation, which in its eyes are a matter of faith, not reason. And so, the philosophers toil away in vain, purporting to desire to make sense of everything, even when their attempts to do so are bound to fail. It all makes sense, including why philosophers should waste their time on doing metaphysics in the name of seeking a sense they know it can never deliver, when we realize that the world is a spectacle whose unending parade of foolish absurdities is orchestrated by the devil, who wants to fascinate us with frivolities meant to distract us from the fact that the thing that matters most in life is following Jesus Christ.

78
Credo quia impossibile

The Christian should not say, with Tertullian, "I believe because it is impossible." He should say, rather, "I believe because it would be impossible for the world to be so absurd otherwise." In other words, only a world in rebellion to God could be so absurd—*ergo*, God.

79
Two, and only two, paths

Every man at heart is a rebel. The question is simply whether he shall choose to rebel against God or the world.

80
The absurdist

Consolation, rebellion, etc.—yes, we will eventually come to Camus.

81

Promising freedom . . .

People so often speak gushingly of freedom. They complain and protest against the societal and historical conditions they believe deny it to them. If they were to be believed, they yearn for nothing more than to be free. And yet, there is no freedom in this life without being liberated from the fear of man. Why, then, do the same people who spend their lives complaining about being unfree not free themselves? Follow Christ, and you will be free. But this is the one thing they will not do! You see, such people don't really want to be free. They only like to think that they do.

82

Time scents

We only become who we are to be when we embrace the fact that the challenges in our life will never change; they remain the same because they're ours, because they're God's way of refining us into the individual he would have us be.

83

Ephemerality

The generations fall like the snowflakes. They flutter for a moment, succeeding one another, only to vanish. I would be driven to despair if I didn't believe that the Lord cares as much for the snowflakes as he does the sparrows.

84

A thought-experiment to dilate the heart

Live in such a way that when you die all those who loved you needn't have the slightest worry that you've been lost to perdition.

85

Life is short, life is long, and then you die

The whole of an entire life is itself short. This is why we say, quite correctly, that it is but a breath. Yet at the same time, there are countless times—moments of boredom, of pain, of loneliness, of bereavement, of sorrow—that are almost unbearable precisely because they feel so extended so as to persist forever. It is not that one truth regarding time must be rejected in favor of the other. Nor is it that we are dealing with two times. There is only one time, yet a time that is somehow paradoxically brief despite consisting in a series of moments that themselves feel to stretch on longer than the life they comprise. This paradox of time is just one way in which God attempts to have us acknowledge eternity, that the mystery of our experience of time, at once so brief yet so long, can only be revealed in a time beyond our current conception. We cannot conceive eternity, for time is only a foretaste of it, yet we know it must exist all the same.

86

Christ is Lord

If all you have is time, then you have nothing.

87

Soothing words

Nearly everything that matters most in life goes unsaid, precisely because it needn't ever be said. It needn't be said because it is already understood. Bringing the matter into language is gratuitous because of a shared understanding so basic that words themselves are entirely unnecessary to express or confirm it. One obvious potential exception, of course, is with love. But even when we say "I love you" to the beloved, we always feel the inadequacy of our words, a fact that only reinforces the lesson that most of our relation to others unfolds through a communication that never reaches language. Declaring our love, to continue with the example, only expresses what was already understood far better than our saying so makes it understood. Words float, drift, skim, and glide atop the surface of the deep sea that is the unsaid, even the unsayable. The writer is the one who attempts to put into words so much of what about life remains unsaid. And the Christian who writes is the one who attempts to put into words God's subtle, yet undeniable, unsaid actions in daily life. This is why he writes, to draw attention to what we otherwise might neglect, because we are so used to taking it for granted that we rarely so much as speak about it.

88

Rainy thoughts

The best thoughts are like a summer rain; we feel them brewing from afar before they have arrived.

89
Unstable in all their ways

There is a problem of evil, in a sense, but it is not an indictment of God requiring a theodicy, as the atheists allege. Evil does not put God on trial. To the contrary, we get the world we deserve. Christ has died for our sins, and yet the atheist scorns him. That the atheist wallows in his own evil and then has the temerity to blame God for what he finds to be unjust about the world—could there be any clearer illustration of what St. Paul means by the reprobate mind spoken of in Romans 1?

90
With what measure ye mete, it shall be measured to you again

Many of the same atheists who gleefully invoke the words of Christ, "Judge not, lest ye be judged," to admonish Christians for their purported self-righteous moralism will in the very next breath judge God—here the "New Atheists" come to mind.

91
Repent in ashes

Followed to its end, the true conclusion of the philosophical problem of evil is the same word Nathan spoke to David: "Thou art the man."

92

The existential problem of evil

Ivan Karamazov rejects the world for all its evil. He "returns God his ticket." This rejection of the world is thus rebellion against God. It should be noted that Ivan fails to draw a distinction between evils God wills and those he permits. Camus's rejection of God rests on the same mistake. But their rejection of God, their response to the existential problem of evil, rests on a deeper mistake than that. We have no right to reject God on the basis of the world's suffering, for who has suffered more unjustifiably at the world's hands than the Savior himself who loves us?

93

Zeal preserves us

Live in such a way that even when death extinguishes your sojourn in this life, the fire within you burns on.

94

Peace is near, if we will it

Regret, disappointment, sorrow—so much of this life is suffering that, in a way, life just *is* suffering, and yet, despite that, the greatest cause of pain is above all that this life is all too brief. That man, who is destined to eternal life in Christ if only he should seize it, should instead cling to this life while remaining in darkness, all the while bemoaning that it will come to an end all too soon—what better proof could be adduced to show that man left to himself is fundamentally at war with himself, and so incapable of finding the very peace he claims to seek but doesn't find, only because he does not truly seek it but prefers to be seen by others, just as miserable as himself, as having sought it?

95
Esau's lentils

Anyone who scoffs at the idea that Esau really sold his birthright for a bowl of soup must be willfully blind to the astonishing fact that the world's inanities all around him, which when compared to the importance of eternal life are so insignificant so as to matter less than even a bowl of soup, are somehow treated with such incredible seriousness. People care more about who wins each year's Superbowl than whether or not they themselves will inherit a crown of victory on the Last Day.

96
Axiom #1

What the Holy Scriptures term "gentleness," "meekness," and "self-control," that is to say, the fruits of the Spirit, naturally are ridiculed and deprecated by atheists (here one thinks above all of Nietzsche) as false virtues, as being in fact weaknesses stemming from the *ressentiment* of those too feeble or cowardly to assert themselves openly and truly. What foolishness this is! Those who have so much to say in praise of what they consider to be power do not admit, are too *weak* to admit, that their thirst for the will to power is itself the zenith of powerlessness, for it is always based in an anger that seeks vengeance for whatever slight or wrong of which it perceives itself to have been the victim. What it calls power, then, and what it exhibits in its carnal craze for dominance over others, is really little more than the expression of a wounded vanity, of one too weak and insecure to tolerate a bruise to one's frail ego. The fundamental axiom of existence that this cult of sham power fails to understand? *Rage does not equal power.*

97
Life's contradictions

Time is everything. Time is nothing. Before we know it, this mortal life slips away from us like a wisp of wind.

98

Faith is higher than proof

One can know something without being able to prove it to others. For what does one acquire by proving to others what one already knew aside from the fact that one already indeed knew what one did? And thus it is with God. Knowing God means pressing deeper into the life he has ordained for us. Proving to others that he exists has nothing to do with knowing him. One could spend a whole lifetime attempting to prove God to others and yet never know him for oneself.

99

Always remember!

There is a vast difference between speaking *of* or *about* God and speaking *to* him. Even when we speak outwardly of God to others, we must always be speaking to him within also, for otherwise whatever we might say is in a fundamental sense false.

100

You are no exception

By the time a man reaches old age ("retirement age," as we say), those around him have already begun treating him far differently than how he'd been treated in his prime. They see him as "soon to die." He becomes almost pitiable in their eyes, someone no longer to be taken seriously, for there is no longer anything to be gained from him amid the "dance of life." If he doesn't love God, and if he hasn't lived his life for God, everything for which he had striven is revealed to have been comical—vain, vulgar, embarrassing. Those who dismiss him as now useless, of course, do not see themselves as always already dying; they don't see that in a way they are in the very same position as the old man who they view as dispensable. Their lives are no less absurd than the old man who lived for the world but now has nothing to show for it. In time, the same lust of the flesh, lust of the eyes, and pride of life that governed his life will be shown to have governed theirs. Only if we can free ourselves from such delusion and see that we ourselves are "soon to die" will we not suffer the fate of having to recognize at the end of our own life that we were foolish for thinking it possible to be anything worthwhile without God.

101

Faith according to Kierkegaard's formulation of despair

"Be yourself." So you ask: "But who else could I be?" In this life, it is possible to be an infinite number of variations of one's false self. One only becomes who one is by being the one God wills one to be.

102

The doctrine of intentionality

The phenomenological doctrine of intentionality, that all consciousness is consciousness of something, that every act of mind has its object, is probably far more complicated than how it is ordinarily understood. In ordinary life, we do not simply perceive any one thing, remember just one thing, imagine one particular thing, or hope for one thing alone. We perceive many objects—a situation, a scene, in fact. Likewise, we remember much at once, imagine many things at once, hope for a number of things at once. More to the point, we perceive, remember, imagine, and hope together, such that they blend together in one experience that is always shifting. When I perceive, my perception is inflected by what I imagine, and what I imagine is shaped by what I remember, and what I perceive, imagine, and remember are all inflected by what I hope. This is the flux of consciousness. Phenomenology attempts to organize this flux by tracing all the laws that determine how the varieties of conscious experience can come to coalesce, yet if we never learn to turn all our thoughts back to God, then we are truly lost in thought.

103

The man at the mall

Augustine remarks somewhere that those who are less fortunate than ourselves may serve as a reminder of thanksgiving for all that we have. For example, you see a young man who is crippled. It is a Saturday afternoon, and he is at the mall with his mother because he has no friends. Is he lonely? Does he feel rejected and pitiful? Observe him and you see his dignity—he is no less satisfied with his life than you are with yours. Then you are struck with the realization that life is a gift. Have we turned him into a spectacle, an object, a mere instrument? But this sort of objection, which takes itself to be the voice of compassion and selflessness, in fact comes from those who have not yet softened themselves to experience the wound of being reminded of their own ingratitude. They still take pride in believing themselves to be above the necessity of learning gratitude in light of the relative struggles of another. When we let ourselves be wounded, struck by our own ingratitude, we see that we ourselves were spiritually crippled, inured to the fact that others may be watching us, just as we had felt compelled to look on this young man, who we sensed had something to teach us. "Let thy light shine," says the Lord.

104

The depths of memory

Have you ever told yourself never to forget some moment for the rest of your life? You search your memory, and you realize that this can't be the whole store of such moments—some have slipped away. Even when we resolve not to forget certain fragments of our life, still sometimes we do. How feeble we are! But even our forgetting might be reason to look on in need of the One who is unforgettable—the God who is always already with us.

105

Faulkner tweaked

The past is never over, for is it never settled.

106

Faulkner tweaked (cont'd)

The past changes with us, just as we change along with it. The nature of betrayal reveals this best. Years of friendship or love can be dashed to pieces in a moment, to the point that whether it was truly friendship or love becomes an open question. The betrayal of someone whom we thought we had known makes us question whether we had ever known him or her at all. The past we thought we knew raises up its heel against us, and we are left wondering what it means at all.

107

Stop worrying

Our minds, which so often are propelled by worry, can turn over some question or problem until we feel that as a result we understand less than ever. Taking this incomprehension itself as a reason to despair, many in response worry even more. But such incomprehension can just as well be a source not of worry but of being unburdened by worry. The believer knows this—when some great mystery perplexes me, and I feel myself up against the limits of my own understanding, I know that God is good—and that is good enough.

108

Little Ludwig

It could be that God has graced us with intelligence solely so that we learn the futility of leaning on our own understanding.

109

The mirror of truth

Others see our faults better than we see them ourselves. Perhaps! Yet this is so precisely because we feel the sting of those faults better than anyone. We choose to remain blind to them because we can't bear to see them, yet we are aware of them all the same.

110

He must increase

If man can't know himself apart from God, this is because of the *imago Dei*. To be made in the image and likeness of God, what does that mean? It means that I know God only insofar as I love him, and I love him only insofar as I obey him. Obeying him—this is how I grow in his likeness, and, becoming more truly myself, I in turn become more and more a reflection of him. Through this likeness, our life becomes a reflection of his image. God doesn't command obedience, that we be good, for any other reason than our own good—that we may know Christ, and so ourselves.

111

As much purity of heart, as much power of vision

Sometimes the transparency of someone's evil is so plain to us (it could be a celebrity, a politician, someone from our daily life) that we marvel how others do not see it also. In such circumstances, we ought to remind ourselves that our perceptiveness is a matter of spiritual discernment, a capacity for judgment that St. Paul says separates the natural man from the spiritual man. As St. Paul says, what the spiritual man sees is seen as "foolishness" to the natural man—today, the latter call the former "paranoid," "crazy," "conspiracy theorist." They say this because they cannot see what we see, and thus they believe that we are the ones "seeing things."

112

They which see may be blind

One mustn't gloat (even silently within oneself) when others much later finally come to see for themselves that which we have seen for ourselves long ago. The same humility that allowed us to see clearly, that explains why we were not deceived by pride, can be destroyed were we to boast in the fact that we saw what others had not seen. From beginning to end, hence, humility must be the principle of our seeing, lest we become blind.

113

Magdalen has fallen

We read an editorial from an online political magazine in which a man who considers himself to be a philosopher offers his thoughts on the latest matter of public controversy (the actual matter at issue is beside the point). Referring in passing to the "intelligent world," the author presents himself as a rare voice of sanity among those who, though educated highly, have lost all common sense and have gone mad. You see, the whole point of the piece, though the author would never dare say it, is to show us that its author is the *truly* intelligent one. That he thinks it worthwhile to mention there being any such thing as an "intelligent world," only underscores that he, even if he has not gone entirely mad like those he criticizes, is stunted spiritually nevertheless. For, at bottom, the world is a lie, and were he to recognize this for himself, he would not be surprised that his peers of the "intelligent world" have gone mad. Indeed, he would laugh at the idea of an "intelligent world," which, strictly speaking, is an oxymoron. Whether we consider the mad of the "intelligent world," or our author, who as the supposed lone dissenter sees their madness but wishes to belong to their world nonetheless, the same underlying foolishness is at work. For if the blind lead the other blind into a ditch, that in no small part is because they don't see that what the world calls wisdom is foolishness.

114
Two forms of gratuity

One way or another, life will be revealed in its gratuitousness—either through a boredom that has nothing to expect but the death it awaits, and thus a boredom that feels this life to be a vapid, pointless gratuitousness, or else through a love that awaits God and thus feels life to be full, pregnant with an abiding joy that is the only proper response to life's greatest gratuity of all, the gift of the promise of eternal life.

115
As much purity of heart, as much power of vision (cont'd)

When we see those who fall for obvious deception, or who believe what is so obviously contrary to all reason and evidence, we can only conclude that their minds are corrupted by some secret vice.

116
Who is the liar?

In order to choose to believe a lie, one must already be lying to oneself.

117
A true life

Even in just ordinary matters of everyday life, the liar hates and fears the truth, because he knows that, if revealed, it will deprive him of his life, a life that, being dependent on lies, is his most cherished lie of all. Yet when it is a matter of a life taken as a whole, this hatred of the truth just described is only more intense—for now the object of hate is not only this or that truth, but the Truth. You cannot lead a life apart from Christ that will not be a lie, for the very decision to reject him is itself already an admission that one is living a lie—why else reject the Truth?

118

Knowing God is personal

There is personal knowledge and there is collective knowledge. If one is wise, has great personal knowledge, and has seen and experienced many things that others have not, one will be astounded by the degree of half-truth, deceit, and deception that passes for truth in the realm of collective knowledge. Very often, this discovery becomes a source of anger and embitterment. If one turns to God, however, then there is peace. One's personal knowledge, which includes knowledge of the world's collective knowledge's falsehoods, can motivate one to press deeper into God rather than bothering with the world's illusions.

119

"Ask anything in my name"

Prayer shows how small we are in comparison to God. How many of our prayers are answered without our knowing? And how many of our prayers that are answered are later forgotten? God gives us what we ask for, and we don't notice because it comes in a form we weren't anticipating, or else we are simply ungrateful by the time it comes. God refuses to give us what we ask for because it would be bad for us or detrimental to us, and we don't appreciate that he protects us from ourselves. When I think on how poorly we appreciate the power of prayer, I am stirred to call out to God for mercy and in gratitude thank him for this mercy, that he forgives my ingratitude for the power of prayer.

120

Breath of God

When you are dry, the winds of inspiration having come to a still, take these doldrums as a moment to listen more intently. Take a deep breath, attend to the silence patiently, and eventually you will hear from the Holy Spirit, who will breathe on you, giving you what it is you are given to say.

121

Write for yourself

Often, writers set out to write for others, and thereby reach no one. A writer must write for himself—in that lies the unusual appeal of the true writer. He expresses his own heart, touching the hearts of those who read him. The first word of advice that should be given to an aspiring writer: "Disregard your audience."

122

Heidegger on conscience

In Division Two of *Being and Time*, Heidegger states that the caller of the call of conscience is anonymous. Anyone who is honest with himself should at that point set the book down. If Heidegger denies that it is the Word alone who speaks to man in the depths, then what else could he possibly say of essential worth that is worth taking seriously? I think this is why many who like Heidegger like him. By deferring to him as a great philosopher, as though he is putting them on the pathway to something essential, they can feel that they are facing up to the fundamental reality of being human when in point of fact they are not. Reading Heidegger, for them, is an escape from being before God.

123

Werhner von Braun's tombstone

"Why is the sky blue?" the child asks. Because of the waters above. How much easier and truer life would be if we had the willingness to answer children's questions with Genesis rather than with the wisdom of the world, what the "intelligent world" *purports* to know.

124

Desiring God

Schopenhauer is quite correct about the perpetual cycle of dissatisfaction besetting what he calls desire. However, rather than seeing its inadequacies as proof that reality were a dark saying, he should instead have understood that God ordains that desire disappoint us so that we might wean ourselves from the false riches of this world and seek him instead. Desire teaches that we should look to him—nothing else!—for satisfaction. This Schopenhauer never did.

125

Christ is the Way

We see others losing their way. How do we know we haven't lost ours also? Only Christ is the Way, for otherwise we will be lost and not even know it.

126

Let my words be not vain

Probably, most writing is a selfish endeavor. Certainly, unless it can be redeemed. But how? Sometimes the very presumption of writing becomes *almost* too much to bear. In the face of its apparent presumptiveness ("Listen everyone, I have something to say"), why then does the writer press on? Herein lies the crucial difference between those who in turn elect to write in vain, which is to say, for themselves in the pride of it, and those who opt to write in humility, which is to say, to communicate what God has called them to say in self-effacement. All writing, in the last analysis, is either undertaken because the writer wills to write in selfish abandon, or else because he empties himself of all pride and lets God attempt to tell him what to say. Oh, Lord, save me from this frivolity! Make my words something more than vain. Let them matter somehow. You have redeemed my life; let my little words be a reflection of your saving power.

127

Still

Although melancholy is rooted in its estrangement from God, at least it has the advantage, spiritually speaking, of not having lost its softness. Cynicism, sarcasm, ironic detachment—these are the surest signs of an even deeper estrangement. Whereas melancholy has not quit caring, the one who is no longer melancholic quit caring about even trying to care. Such nihilism revels in its own destruction. With melancholy, it is different, in that it still countenances the possibility of salvation, for it still wants to be consoled, still wants others to be consoled, still wants to believe that, in the end, all things do indeed work for the good of those who love God. Still, still, still—one must never let go of the *still*, for then one is still not fully lost.

128

Spiritual procrastination is presumption

One of the wickedest tricks that the devil and his demons play on us is to get us to assure ourselves that, though not straightaway, soon we will repent. We know that we are on the wrong path, but we tell ourselves that we will correct our way later. No! Today must be the day of salvation. The moment your heart reminds you that you are on the wrong path, that you have gone astray, that you are walking in darkness, you must part ways with everything that is persuading you to walk that path and come into the light instead. There are people who die completely estranged from God, having led evil lives, without the slightest pang of conscience, without the slightest desire to repent, who in their youth had told themselves that they would only enjoy sin for a season before turning to God later in life.

129

Being true

Analytic philosophers have had much to say about what can be true: sentences, statements, beliefs, judgments, propositions, states of affairs, and so forth. They call such things "truth-bearers." But these same philosophers neglect the fact that *we* are the most important truth-bearers of all. For a life itself can be true or false.

130

You are what you think

Is it so, that the true philosopher thinks only one thought?

131

Philosophy without God

In what does the encounter with God consist—a long line of philosophers has denied that any such revelation occurs, either because there is no God to meet us (Hume, Voltaire, Sartre, etc.) or else because God is wholly transcendent, rendering any possible experience of him impossible (Kant, Janicaud, and then of course a litany of lesser names). This claim bothered me, not only because it seemed to me false—as a matter of experiential fact, we *do* encounter God—but also because of what appeared to me to be the bankruptcy of a philosophy that denies the revelation of God. If there is no God, or God has nothing to contribute to our existence, how vain would philosophy be! It would be an idle diversion from the underlying meaninglessness of existence, the apogee of futility, an exercise in thinking the absurdity of existence despite the very absurdity of doing so.

132

First principles

Any existentialist philosophy truly worthy of the name must begin with the acknowledgment of God.

133

The perversion of philosophy

Atheists will mock the notion that philosophy should be a consolation without noticing that they themselves have twisted it into a pathology.

134

Idealists are the true realists

Nobody is more pragmatic than the sincere idealist, for the ultimate idealist is the one who, in refusing to compromise with the world, remains loyal to God, striving to learn the imitation of Christ. And God, of course, is the one who in the last analysis shall be our judge.

135

Sirach

At the beginning of the Septuagint's Book of Sirach, the writer addresses himself to those who are "addicted to the truth." Ah, one addiction that is not a vice!

136

Know thyself

Until we enter into life in Christ, we don't even know what we desire. We lead a life subject to the ravishes of desire, the heart of which remains obscure to us. Tarkovsky's *Stalker* has shown this.

137

Philosophy of mind without God

When I initially began investigating what phenomenology calls the "first-person perspective," I was struck by how drastically the prevailing materialist and naturalistic dogmas of the philosophy of mind had distorted even the most self-evident experiential facts of consciousness. In the name of studying consciousness, these philosophers of mind have contorted consciousness beyond all recognition. When I asked *why* they would do this, the true motivation for purveying such shameless obfuscations, I suspected, was to ignore the one experiential fact they feared the most, namely, that God's claim on man's existence has made itself known.

138

Being-towards-death

At the end of Division One of *Being and Time*, Heidegger notes that the existential analytic appears to end in aporia. The philosophical interrogation of Dasein aims to bring the whole of Dasein's existence into view, yet that effort seems to be thwarted inasmuch as existence is subject to death. Heidegger's introduction of authenticity, formulated in terms of being-towards-death, seeks to resolve this paradox by insisting that Dasein can be grasped as a whole in anxiety.

139

Being-towards-death (cont'd)

How, then, do we bring our life as a whole into view? Following someone like Ricœur, here philosophy introduces narrativity as a solution. Because the present appears to us on the basis of a past that we reimagine according to a future that we hope to experience, we unify life as a whole in virtue of narrative. But regardless of whatever narrative we go on to form, life fails to cohere meaningfully, for this life of care, this life that lives burdened by worry and trouble, labors under the incessant weight of a death that remains incomprehensible to it. Only Christ, who is the Life, can overcome the unintelligibility of a life that otherwise will be held hostage to the power of death's senselessness.

140

Sartre's error

The atheistic existentialists, like Sartre, who claim selfhood is a nullity, are only partially correct. They are correct that daily life is performative. In that respect, it is true that we are not what we are. As Sartre says, I am a waiter in the mode of not being one. But as Sartre himself notes, even if I am nothing but my worldly possibilities, there always remains a dimension of myself that lies beneath whatever worldly possibility I press into. This is where its account of subjectivity goes wrong. For when it grants the last word to nothingness, it makes the mistake of thinking existence in terms of exteriority only. Rather than seeking God in the interiority of oneself, it seeks itself in the world's exteriority. The nothingness it claims to discover lying at the heart of human existence, thus, is merely the surface of a far deeper form of selfhood it never brings into view, owing to it being blind to being before God.

141

Whence phenomenology?

"But then this is all mysticism," you will say! So be it: the experiential facts call for a phenomenology of mysticism.

142

The vanity of authenticity

If, as we maintain, the truth of selfhood resides in interiority, not in the world's exteriority, then we must go farther than Adorno. Where Adorno criticizes what he calls Heidegger's "jargon of authenticity," we must criticize its vanity. Living authentically is futile, pointless, useless, vain because it expressly deprives itself of the only basis on which a life can be affirmed: God's love.

143

Leuven

I give a paper, to which an excited audience member insists, "You must read Jan van Ruusbroec!" On the train, in a moment of ecstatic joy, it comes to me. Without having read Ruusbroec, I have said what Ruusbroec had said. It's a moment of liberation: no longer is philosophy an attempt to be original. The truth is immemorial. What is needed is merely to reveal what others have known too.

144

Religious pluralism

The trouble with the form of religious pluralism that treats all religions as equally valid expressions of a noumenal divine transcendence is that it thereby forecloses the position that any one of them is true on its own terms. Only exclusivism does the Absolute justice.

145

Kierkegaard's insight

When Kierkegaard insists that "truth is subjectivity," what he really means to emphasize is that the truth is not merely propositional. The truth is not just a state of affairs that we either affirm or not. The Truth is a Person, thus whether we are in the truth or not is entirely dependent on whether our life is itself a reflection of that fact.

146

Contemplation

Many of the greatest Christian mystics have stressed the wonders of the contemplative life. For when we contemplate God, our soul takes flight, and, like the birds of the air who receive everything they need from God, who stretches out the heavens, so too we rest content in the present. Of course, there is nothing novel about this observation. Richard of St. Victor, Kierkegaard, even Merton, have said so. All the better! The most important, most profound truths needn't be original.

147

Ars divina

If we understand why St. Paul in Romans observes that through created visible things we know of their Creator, we will also understand why so much has rightly been made of the idea that creation is *ars divina*. When creation itself is appreciated as being the creative expression of God, light is shed on the significance of our own human capacity to create art. God, who in this respect is the supreme artist, has endowed us with the ability to create art also. Whether it be in music, literature, poetry, painting, sculpture, or architecture, our creative acts reflect the mark of the supreme artist who has made us in his image. Despite this similarity between God and us, there of course is an infinite qualitative difference. When we create, we do not create *ex nihilo*. Moreover, no matter how relatively perfect the work we create is, we, for our own part, never find complete satisfaction in it. With God, it is different, I believe. Always sustaining his creatures, God finds constant enjoyment in his creation. With us, not so. From the initial birth pangs of a work's conception, from the moment of inspiration, to the hard work of giving it shape, to the temporary enjoyment of reaching the stage where we know we have something worth having begun on, till its final completion when we are at last finished with it, there is never complete satisfaction in the labor of what we create. The supreme artist ensures that we never find rest in the work of our own hands so that we might never forget that created things will never be a substitute for the satisfaction to be found in God alone.

148

Our hands

Said otherwise, even man's highest callings and his greatest accomplishments, those brought about by the labor of his own hands, are testaments to his fundamental impoverishment. Every work of our own hands is a cry for our Creator to complete us in a way nothing else can.

149

Take a breath

After an intense period of intellectual productivity, in which you have had much to think and you realize that you are pleased with yourself, turn your attention back to the Scriptures so that you don't become enamored with your own thoughts and grow vain in your own imagination.

150

We who are overcomers

The will is stronger than any emotion. No matter the circumstances in which we find ourselves, no matter how despondent, dejected, or disillusioned those who persecute us would have us wish to feel, they have no power over us. God is our high tower, which is why the way we respond is up to us.

151

On evil

Evil must be understood as unnatural, as a monstrous disfigurement of man's proper condition.

152

On evil (cont'd)

Fichte attributes evil to the two causes of selfishness and cowardice. This is a persuasive explanation of evil so long as one understands it in an expansive sense, as anything falling short of what moral duty demands. It must be emphasized, however, that there are degrees of evil (even perhaps discrete stages), and when one considers the most monstrous evils, mere selfishness or cowardice no longer suffice as an explanation. Such evils do not just fall short of what moral duty demands—they knowingly flout duty and scorn the good for the very sake of doing so. This evil is sadistic, destructive, diabolic—for it enjoys the thrill of transgression.

153
On the side of the angels

In this life, the Lord allows us to be on the "side of the angels." What an unspeakable sorrow that so many not only refuse to be so but instead choose to side with the demons.

154
Judas #2

Anyone who can look upon all of this world's evils and not submit to Christ is a traitor to the human race. Such people are like a prisoner who joins up with the guards, taking relief in having become one of the tormentors.

155
Cloud of witnesses

If we will to resist evil, we must never let suffering embitter us. The Lord suffered far more afflictions—and was blameless!—than we do. The Lord endured it all. So must we.

156
Evil is inhuman

If man's nature had truly been corrupted by the fall, as the western doctrine of original sin maintains, then the psychopath, who is the embodiment of evil, would not also be the paragon of *inhumanity*. There is nothing natural or endemic about evil—it is pure perversion.

157

Never alone, never forsaken

The solitude of persecution reminds us that, in the end, God alone will be there for us. In this way, even those who wish to do us harm only draw us closer to what we need more than anything else—God's love, his kindness, his mercy. Others may not weep with us, but the Lord counts each and every one of our tears. You are never alone, never forsaken—to me, this is the heart of the gospel.

158

A new name

Most days, I don't even need to know my own outward name. Nobody calls to me but you.

159

Joy

Joy comes in the epiphany that there needn't be any reason for it besides existence itself.

160

To be a bee

Dostoevsky condemns the socialist utopia imagined by his day's revolutionaries as an "anthill," a society in which the humanity of individuals would be sacrificed on the altar of a perverse conception of social justice. The metaphor is correct, insofar as Dostoevsky intends it. But there is a wholly different way of thinking the similarity between man and the ant. For the Bible does liken the affairs of men to the ant. Famed for their industriousness, the ants work individually for the good of their collective. However, if one wishes to distance oneself from any possible negative connotation associated with the anthill, we might compare the affairs of men instead to the bee hive. (Rilke, for one, speaks of us being "bees of the invisible.") There are worker bees, and there are warrior bees. I am a warrior bee. What a delight it was, then, to find in St. Paul mention of being a "soldier for Jesus Christ." There is no higher calling, it seems to me, in one man's little individual existence than to be a warrior bee, to be a warrior for Christ.

161

The others

If you have a vision of what God gives you to accomplish, expect naysayers to dissuade you from trying. You must understand these attacks as affirmations that you are indeed on the right path.

162

Life's measure

The imitation of Christ is the true measure for life. It is not an external principle or image that lies outside us. For when we emulate Christ, it is by him working in us. Our lives, in turn, become an outward reflection of him: a visible image of the invisible image that forms and animates it.

163

Taking heart

Are you tired? Feeling weak? When you believe yourself to be at the limits of your power, take heart and take a breath, for there is always a greater strength to be had should you let the power of Christ strengthen you.

164

Passing through

When John the Baptist left the cities to dwell alone in the wilderness, he recognized that, in a way, the world as a whole is not our home. May we learn the lesson John learned, that in this life we must live in anticipation of the kingdom of heaven.

165

House of mirrors

Dante equates being lost in the world to being forlorn in a dark wood. I sometimes think a more fitting metaphor for such a condition is to analogize the world as a house of mirrors in which we are constantly being tempted to mistake ourselves with the distorted reflections we encounter all around us. For we are always emulating something, a measure, an ideal, an image. Human existence is inescapably mimetic. Satan knows this better than anyone, which is why he crafts innumerable false images, hoping that we will conform ourselves to anything besides Christ.

166

Wash me clean

What is sweeter than to feel the goodness within oneself, to know that, purified of one's former evils, God has renewed us to innocence through a second birth in him? People can spend an entire life searching in vain for satisfaction and fulfillment in everything else, never accepting that being in the state of grace is to be prized above all else.

167

Weightless

Why the evilest of men refuse to repent was mystifying until I accepted that they must fundamentally *enjoy* the misery of being lost. They cling to their wretched condition, despite all of its anxieties, sorrows, and shames, because they'd be nothing without the occasional exhilaration they experience from scorning God.

168

"I don't believe in a judgment"

Atheism offers no hope but the hope that there be no afterlife. This is the unintentional confession of atheism's inward evil, that atheists must hope there is no God to judge them for the life they have led ignoring him. I feel like I have already said this. Well, say it again!

169

A footnote to Plato

Ever since Plato, many philosophers have had their suspicions that the arts are in some way evil, insofar as they promote illusion, fantasy, or even outright falsehood. But if the plastic arts were cause for concern enough, the invention of film, which for the first time allows for the reproduction of reality, thereby permits the substitution of reality by an image of it. Although perhaps the medium itself is not inherently evil (is an image, in that respect a representation of reality in its absence, a privation in the Augustinian sense?), many of those who make films have used the medium as a way to become a demiurge. One thinks here of Béla Tarr's *The Turin Horse*.

170

Aesthetic perception

A beautiful painting (and a painting *should* be beautiful!) discloses the glory of being, the splendor of the world when it is seen properly as God's creation. On the visible canvas before us, we see the inward glory of things. The aesthetic experience of appreciating a painting is similar to how in the encounter with a visible face, we can perceive the other's soul.

171

Truthfulness in literature

A work of literature that is too descriptive robs the reader of the opportunity to exercise his imagination. In order to depict a world successfully, there must be a sufficiently indeterminate and ambiguous horizon structuring the events and places described, otherwise the "world" of the novel will be artificial. The novelist's task is not to be the demiurge of his own fictional creation, but to disclose what God has created by reawakening in his reader an attention to the richness of what he typically ignores.

172

The gift of hands

Le don des mains, an expression we owe to Emmanuel Housset, distills perfectly the essence of our being made in the image of God. The human hand, carnal and material, is infused with the spiritual capacity for love, expression, creativity, and so forth. By the works and gestures of our hands, we confess that God has entrusted us with the responsibility to make our lives a reflection of the gift of life that we have received at his hands.

173

The goddess trap

I am glad to have been considered dreamy rather than edgy. Even during the years when I was lost, I had not given up the search.

174

Kandinsky's blue

Though they remain famous for other reasons, Newton and Goethe are still mentioned for their respective theories of color. But we mustn't forget Kandinsky! To be sure, Kandinsky does not offer us a scientific theory of color perception. Instead, he offers us something far more essential, in short, insight into the spiritual reality of color. He holds, for instance, that blue is the color of eternity. Anyone who has looked out at the emerald Aegean will have seen for himself what Kandinsky means, for the blue expanse of the sea before us and sky above is the nearest thing we can know to Eden in this life.

175

Yupon St

Chartreuse, the color, not the liquor, will for me always be associated with the Word. While on solitary summer walks at night along empty streets beneath yellow streetlights shimmering through the curling southern oaks, there was the chorus of cicadas, crickets, and frogs reverberating in the humidity. But more than that, I could hear your voice calling to me through the light.

176
Either/Or

How is phenomenology to approach revelation? In the end, Heidegger never really did, for his philosophy of Dasein is methodologically atheist. As for someone like Ricœur, he promises to get there, albeit eventually, through the "long way" of hermeneutics. Ricœur's philosophy, however, never reached the phenomenon of the revelation of Jesus Christ any more than did Heidegger's. The promised land always remains only in sight. (And when one reads his unpublished working notes, *Living Up to Death*, one is struck by the fact that Ricœur's own personal faith was far less firm than one might have thought it would be.) In order for a phenomenology of revelation to be true to the phenomenon, it must either accept Christ immediately, without condition, or else admit that it has rejected him. There can be no neutral middle ground, no "lukewarm" phenomenology.

177
Lacoste's insight

In short, any description of existence ignoring the appearing of God will be incorrect.

178

The atheist's parlor trick

The atheist's rejoinder is predictable: "But why? Why the god of Jesus Christ? Why not another god?" (To begin with, we can't help but notice that the atheist loves to lower case the "g.") In any case, what really in effect is being demanded here? *Prove to me that Jesus is the Christ.* But this is as ridiculous as it is disingenuous. Why must *I* prove to someone that Christ is who Christ himself says he is? Is the thought truly supposed to be that I can somehow persuade the atheist that God is the God of Jesus Christ? And the implication is that if I can't demonstrate so to the atheist's satisfaction, then Jesus in fact is not the Christ, or that at least there is no reason to believe he is? This is all smoke and mirrors—Christ is who he says he is (or he isn't), and whether I or anyone else can persuade the atheist of it is beside the point. You see, this is the fundamental dishonesty of atheism. It pretends to argue with the believer, when really it argues with Christ.

179

When there were payphones

No matter where I find myself, still there are moments when an ordinary fall day calls me back to San Jose. Just as winter is the season of death, and so fall its premonition, that the latter should remind me of California makes sense, since that was the place of my youth, which, now behind me, is dead save for the memory of it. But the way the particularities of these mundane fall scenes—half-barren trees, hazy sunlight streaking through the solemn clouds, crisp air—awaken the past in me goes deeper than recollection. Without intending it, I think I am young again, but then all the faces of old friends and others whom I haven't thought of in years pass before me, and I realize that the world I knew has faded away like all the leaves drifting down around me, blown away, gone with the wind.

180

Sea thoughts

Last night, I had the strongest urge to visit the sea. The thought of walking the beach, of seeing the waves, of smelling the salt, of hearing the gulls, was almost enough to convince me that inspiration itself demanded I go. I was unable to go, so then I was left to wonder whether I should regret that fact. Undoubtedly, what I write now will not be the same as what I would have written had I gone. I know there are thoughts that would have come to me at the sea that will never reveal themselves elsewhere—where exactly do these unthought thoughts reside?

181

Abraham cannot speak

Belief in God transcends the space of reasons, yet it is not irrational, as commonly suggested. The evidence for faith is ineffable, yes, but that is quite fitting—no words of ours can demonstrate God, for all of our words are always already but a response to he who is the Word.

182

You said my name

The blessedness of having encountered God's presence more fully than is ordinarily the case is enough to nourish a faith for a lifetime. I can say so from experience. If you have never had such an experience yourself of this indescribable joyful bliss, I can only attest that the hope within me lies on firmer ground than does my belief that here is a hand (G. E. Moore), or that the world has existed for more than ten minutes (Russell). Faith in God is not really ultimately a matter of whether we have certitude or not, for it is a matter of coming to know God better and better by loving him. That said, it is a testimony of his love that he will provide the certitude we think we need, if we indeed need it. (And if you lack such certitude because you have yet to experience it and you think you need it, you are mistaken for that very reason, for God has decided that you are strong enough to pursue him without it!)

183

The Mercure on Merton

God works in such mysterious ways that sometimes he accomplishes his own purposes by using those who aim to oppose him. Nowhere is this more apparent than in persecution. For instance, those who count me as their enemies expend more effort monitoring my work's progress than they do making any headway with their own. I have observed that as my work has developed and progressed, what others have termed a "cabal" of my detractors has only become increasingly invested in stopping it. As a result of their various tactics, which have grown increasingly desperate and unhinged, a divinely appointed cycle of persecution has set in: the longer they attempt to ignore and destroy my work, the more diligently I have in response focused on continuing to produce more of it. I have strived to forget about them, losing myself in my work. It is the opposite with them. Years have passed, and they have nothing to show for themselves. To think they truly expected me to sell my soul just to be able to write book reports on Heidegger's concept of death: sad!

184

Our reader's expectations

There is a certain kind of reader today who would be surprised to find a work such as this one not contain a single reference to Slavoj Žižek. There: may the reader be pleased!

185

Ghost monster

A close friend once said of me in my presence that I was a "ghost monster." What he meant, I see now, was that a sense of how I would perceive his actions, were I there to witness them, haunted him. I was an inconvenient reminder that what he was transforming into was something at once as unrecognizable as it was wrong. Needless to say, it wasn't long before we went our separate ways. Sometimes being a true friend means doing right by him, even if you know that means he will hate you for it. In this comparatively puny act of self-sacrificial love, you gain a glimpse into Christ's own sacrificial death for us.

186

Los Osos

One of the sweetest experiences of what is also a fond childhood memory has been returning home and walking amid the Eucalyptus groves at the beach. These trees have always been a haven. Their sweet fragrance assuages the longing for eternity.

187

Punished by their sins

"Life's not fair"—*au contraire*! Though they often escape social and civil ramifications for their misdeeds, even the most powerful of the wicked get away with nothing, for sin itself is its own punishment.

188

The world is a cold place

The more fully I began to ascertain the world's monstrous indifference to me as an individual, indeed to each and every one of us, the more I appreciated the good news of Christ's love.

189

The obfuscations of method

There is an objection to the "theological turn" of phenomenology, according to which anything besides methodological atheism violates the Husserlian measure of *Evidenz*. On this view, the phenomenological reduction, properly understood, turns on the practice of epistemological ascesis: in short, a phenomenological judgment must abstain from making any claim for which there is not intuitive givenness. Now God, so this objection goes, is not given in *Evidenz*, therefore phenomenology must bracket the question of God. In short, metaphysical humility demands that we set aside the question of God. This self-professed ascetic attitude, however, which presents itself as a paragon of epistemic humility, is, on the contrary, extraordinarily audacious, for it claims to know that God is incapable of revealing himself. Thus, in the name of philosophical humility, it presumes to have silenced God. Only a deeply corrupted mind could ever devise such an obvious sleight of hand and then dress it up in the guise of philosophical "method"!

190

The God who comes to mind

NB: St. Paul says the carnal mind is enmity against God. In his commentary on Romans, Pelagius, for his part, notes that a reprobate mind is one that merely desires not to know God, a mind that wishes to keep God out of mind. When appreciated in that light, the philosophical imperative to bracket God in the name of phenomenological method proves simply to be a convoluted attempt to avoid acknowledging God. Surely, no phenomenological philosophy worthy of the name should be an exercise in reprobation! Hence, the appearing of God cannot be ignored in the name of philosophical method.

191

The rule must be: always showing, never telling

I once wrote a review of *The Oxford Handbook of the History of Phenomenology*. In doing so, I was reminded of the value of familiarizing oneself with the history of phenomenology and that one always has more to learn from what others in the tradition have themselves said. Ultimately, however, when doing phenomenological philosophy, one's task is to describe what appears rather than summarize what those who made that task their work said in doing so.

192

Cricket

According to Lewis Carroll's White Queen, in Wonderland one must believe six impossible things before breakfast. Back at the college, the biggest howler of all was the logical contradiction that something's being published doesn't entail that it is publishable.

193

Memento mori

Over the course of this writing, I have periodically been assailed intensely by a feeling of sadness about death. I am not afraid to die, I don't think, for I know that with God's mercy, I shall be with Christ forever. And I accept, as best I can, that everything I currently love will eventually perish—wife, parents, friends, pets. I know that for those who die in Christ, death will have been conquered, and there is only reason for hope and gratitude. Yet in the meantime, I cannot help but feel the sadness of creation all around me, that the whole of it groans in anticipation of finally being redeemed and freed from this curse of death.

194

To die

Plato's Socrates avers that philosophy is preparing for death. In the time shortly before taking the hemlock, he gives an account of how he has lived the examined life, which is to say, has thought existence in light of living before death. The modern philosophers worth reading—Husserl, Heidegger, and Levinas, among others—understand philosophy in this Socratic fashion, inasmuch as they understand it as a practice for dying, as an attempt to give sense to death, even if, in doing so, we come to realize that we must acknowledge death remains mysterious, if not wholly unintelligible. Death—in one regard the ultimate phenomenon of life, for it is what makes life finite and thus fragile—is a *non*-phenomenon. First, because I do not know what it holds for me, do not know what it is like to be dead, until it has arrived and I have died. Until it has given itself fully, which will mean I am no longer in any position to speak of it in this world, in this life, I am left only to anticipate what it will entail for me. That anticipation in the face of death is mortality—anticipating the meaning of the death that haunts the time we are given. Second, because the death of others is not something we experience directly for ourselves. It is probably true that, in this life, we make most sense of death, so far as that is possible, through the experience of the death of others. In this respect, there are three dimensions to death. There is the sense of death in general—what results from the relative indifference we feel towards the death of those we either don't know at all, or at least don't know well enough to care deeply about. This is the kind of rapport with death that comes from the news story—a car accident, a shooting, in short, someone's dying in the sense Heidegger would call inauthentic, the "everyone dies" mode of encountering death by keeping it at arm's length. Then there is the death of others that is more personal—the death of the friend, the family member, or even an acquaintance. In this second form, the world changes through the other's absence. The view they once took on the world is now absent. And we feel that lack. This only adds to death's mystery—for in this case, the other, as Housset says in his fragility book, is characterized by an "enigmatic presence," at once "still there" yet "definitively absent." These two first forms of the other's death only underscore that there is a human commonality, a bond, a shared solidarity, in death. The point can be underscored through an eidetic variation. Were, for instance, I to be immortal, but no one else, or were everyone else to be immortal, but not me, our experience would be entirely different from how it is, given the fact that each and every one of us, without exception, is mortal. This solidarity in our shared mortality doesn't begin to take the sting out of death, however, when it comes to the third way in which the death of the other reveals itself to me. For, finally, there is the death of the beloved, the dearest of all. In the grief brought on by the death of the beloved, it is not just that the world changes, as in the former case, but that it changes entirely, for everything is now a mere reminder of the other's absence. Here, nothing short of the hope of being reunited in the next life can console our grief. This is why, although it is true that death does not mean we are isolated subjects, in the sense of being a Cartesian ego or an egocentric narcissist, we are nonetheless alone. In the end, we die alone, and we bear our grief alone. I think this is so because God has seen fit that, in our pain, in the loss of the beloved, we should turn to him—the One who ensures that love indeed is stronger than death.

195

Dilapidation

An otherwise robust building will dilapidate more rapidly than it would otherwise have as soon as it is uninhabited. And here it is not a question of the lack of maintenance. I mean simply that the mere presence of a living human has the power to maintain a space's longevity. The second that human life leaves, the place begins to deteriorate without it. It is as if the human person is the soul of the structure. I suppose there is a sign here in such dereliction of what awaits us all personally. For when our soul abandons the body, the body itself will quickly waste away.

196

Hyperion

"To feel one moment as if one were everything and the world nothing, then to feel as if the world were everything and one were nothing"—this line of Hölderlin routinely springs to mind when I think on death. Robinson, for her part, says something similar in *Gilead*, when the story's narrator, the elderly pastor John Ames, writes of our "mortal insufficiency to the world" and the "world's mortal insufficiency to us." All the years before my birth, all the years sure to follow after my death—what meaning there is to this life, is it not clear that its ultimate significance must reside in something lying beyond my time in the world, beyond the time that leads to death?

197

The unimaginable

The reality of one's death is unimaginable. It is incomprehensible. I know that I am going to die, but I do not really believe it. I can only cling to Christ, hoping that I meet it well, hopeful that through the great mercy of God, all shall be okay.

198

The school of death

According to Shestov, for whom Greek wisdom and biblical revelation were so fundamentally opposed, all true philosophy is not a *meditatio vitae* but rather a *meditatio mortis*. Yet, as he himself suggests, meditation on death needn't lead to despair. Even death can be received as a gift, for the memory of it is what frees us from the illusions of this transient life that would otherwise cloud our vision, all the illusions, that is, that would blind us to the reality that, because our time is short and we are headed toward death, life itself must become a preparation for what lies beyond it. Death frees us, if we face up to it honestly, for then it compels us to seek salvation in Christ who is Life.

199

Camus's quasi-Gnosticism

Metaphysical rebellion, as Camus understands it, is in part a revolt against the world—it is a refusal to accept death and all the senseless suffering of an unjust and cruel world. Camus is a rationalist in that he never abandons the view that we ought to believe only what can be justified by reason—for him, this excludes belief in God, which, as a matter of faith, qualifies as irrational, and hence as a mere form of illusory consolation. In this way, he is a strange blend of Kant and Freud—Kantian in that he thinks the limits of reason forbid an experience of God, Freudian in that he thinks the belief in God, despite the supposed lack of such experience is rooted in wish-fulfillment. This leads him to his fundamental criticism of Dostoevsky—namely, that Dostoevsky chooses to believe in immortality in order to avoid the conclusion that life *is* absurd and meaningless. Camus, however, who is so perceptive when it comes to identifying the world's various injustices and absurdities, makes the mistake of seeing belief in God as little more than a metaphysical consolation. In point of fact, it is the Christian who knows better than anyone, even better than the absurdist, how truly absurd the world can be. He knows this better than anyone, for the kinder he becomes, the more others scorn him as cruel; the gentler he becomes, the more others reproach him as harsh; the humbler he becomes, the more others charge him of pride; the more selfless he becomes, the more others accuse him of selfishness; the more suffering he endures in quiet patience, the more others indict him of self-pity; far be it from fleeing from an experience of the world's absurdity into the arms of a consoling illusory belief, it is obedience to Christ that leads him willingly to incur degrees of absurdity of which even the unbelieving absurdist could not begin to dream. Camus is to be admired for his quasi-Gnosticism, since that aspect of temperament led him honestly to catalog the multitudinous ways in which the world is indeed meaningless were there no God. But it is a tragedy that, in revolting against the world as he did, he never made the further movement of living out life in Christ. In the end, Camus rejects God because he blames God, rather than the world, for everything he understandably found intolerable about the latter. He *revolted* against the world, but he did not *overcome* it. Only through Christ can one do that successfully.

200

We see no more than what we want to see

"On course but destinationaless"—A. R. Ammons's turn of phrase describes his taking walks along the New Jersey shore bluffs. Of course, he means something deeper by the expression. For in likening these meanderings to the journey itself of life, Ammons means to suggest that we are always on the move, despite the fact that there is never any ultimate end to which we're travelling. I must disagree with the conclusion he draws. Stand on the bluffs and look out to the sea—then you will see that there is a destination, the kingdom of heaven, which lies on the hitherside of death, this life's final horizon.

201

Experiential truths

John, "the most beloved disciple," states that Christ is the Light who lights everyone who comes into the world. This is what makes the denial of Christ so egregious—in denying him, unbelievers estrange themselves from the heart of their humanity. I could go on and on about how, as someone like Michel Henry has shown, this is the case, but ultimately everyone is already in a position to acknowledge that truth for himself, if he is willing. A phenomenology of life like Henry's cannot compel others to be honest about the experiential facts; it can only highlight what others can, and should, already recognize for themselves. Phenomenological philosophy of this kind, that takes seriously its vocation to proceed in the presence of God, doesn't show us anything we've never seen before for ourselves; it reminds us of what we've tried to forget, it brings to our attention what we'd been failing to attend to properly.

202

Said otherwise

A true work of phenomenology is a work of truth because it encourages us not to lie to ourselves.

203
Alpha and Omega

Even amid the train of a philosophical thought refusing to acknowledge so, Christ remains Alpha and Omega.

204
Doing phenomenology

Names, names, names—in academic circles, that is all one encounters any time one tries to think or to write. "Yes, but have you considered . . . ?" "What about the objection from . . . ?" "Have you read . . . ?" Yes, I have read! In truth, I have read far more than most of those who ask me whether I have read. Thinking I could find a haven from all this pretending, I turned to phenomenology. After all, the movement's greats are expressly held up for having said the same. Husserl, for example, speaks of the ethical imperative of taking self-responsibility for one's beliefs. And Heidegger says so much against conformism. But then when one attempts to think for oneself, to write what one believes to have seen for oneself, the others resent one for it, and in the name of phenomenology! What Kierkegaard said of the theology professor applies just as well to the phenomenology professor.

205
Christian existentialism

One authors all manner of works: monographs, novels, book reviews, journal articles, and so forth. And then, virtually no one engages with a single argument from any of it. What is the essential claim I've aimed to make? That we are always already before God, and that there is no justifiable basis on which anything done in the name of philosophy can deny it. *To think existence we cannot but think on God.* This is why I have now decided to write aphorisms instead. I see no reason to repeat at length all the arguments those whom disagree with me have ignored. Better simply to declare what I believe in a fragmentary way that dispenses with the expectation of any systematic reply.

206

Hell is bad people

When I saw in Italy how the others spoke of Marion so cruelly and malevolently in his absence, I saw that God was right to have protected me from what would have been the error of having bothered to seek their approval. For one can accomplish more than they ever could dream of achieving for themselves, and still they will sneer.

207

Giardino di Boboli

I stood beholding the ancient grandeur of Florence from a royal garden, and I suppose I felt then as Tarkovsky had felt in Italy. Exiled, ready to return home.

208

To drink of the Lord's cup

When we meditate deeply upon the horrifying fact that this world tortured and murdered Christ, we can have no illusions that the world, which has hated him first, will hate anyone who follows him also. The honor that comes from God only—it entails being hated by the world. We mustn't despair, however. This is why the Lord himself in the Beatitudes says that we must leap for joy when we are persecuted for his name's sake. For why should anyone desire glory and honor from a world that has spilled the precious blood of the Savoir? Although there is much else wrong with his theology, Spurgeon understood this truth well.

209

Cinema Paradiso

The postmodernist notion that art is somehow higher than life, or that life would not be worth living without art, or that art in a way redeems life, has merit. What I cannot accept is that morality must go out the window in order to produce great art. Alfredo should not have lied to Salvatore.

210

"Give us Barabbas!"

If St. Paul had read aloud to a crowd of listeners the long list of afflictions and persecutions he had endured for the sake of the gospel, I imagine that someone standing there would have sneered, chiding him for complaining. Nowadays, no doubt such a person would wave away all such suffering as being the mark of someone with a "persecution complex." You see, in this life, you either suffer for Christ or else you become someone indifferent and callous to those who do.

211

Those who hate those who follow after good

It is bad enough to refuse to pick up one's own cross and follow Christ. But then to mock and disparage and deride those who do, that truly is the spirit of antichrist.

212

Don't be fake

A large extent of social dynamics is about reaching a result, truth be damned, that will ensure those involved won't feel badly about themselves. This is why the Scriptures routinely condemn the norms of banal daily life, with all its flattery, its disingenuousness, its cowardice, its hypocrisy, its selfishness. If you are in some sense an outsider, even a pariah, be grateful, for the Lord has blessed you by delivering you from falsehood.

213
Demas #2

"Love not the world nor the things in the world," "Friendship with the world is enmity with God," "The world will hate you as it has hated me," etc.—these Scriptures are so simple, so clear, that even a child can understand by them that the kingdoms of this world belong to Satan. And what do the theologians do? They run off to write books extolling the world, claiming that faith ought to affirm the very world that Christ and the apostles command us to overcome. They are worse than Demas because they don't even have the integrity to acknowledge their betrayal for what it really is.

214
Camus's piety

In an important sense, thus, Camus the atheist has more reverence for humanity than the professed Christian mentioned above. Camus finds the world's suffering and injustice to be intolerable insults to human dignity. His mistake, of course, is that in this ethical zeal, this strong hatred of evil, he revolts against the world by also rejecting God. With the lukewarm Christian, it is worse. This type will actually go so far as to affirm the world someone like Camus rightly revolts against, and this despite being expressly commanded over and over and over again to reject the world by the very God he purports to follow! Camus languishes in a hinterland, neither at home in the world nor reconciled to the God who commands us to hate it. But the fake Christian, who counsels us to love the world despite all its evil and injustice, denies the Lord he professes to love. In this respect, Camus came much closer to embodying Christ's teachings than do the world-lovers who claim to follow Christ but don't.

215

Golden calves

Pretty much everything that commands most people's attention, news of current events, foreign affairs, elections, sports, celebrities, this controversy or that controversy, is an obvious diversion from death. How fitting that those who claim not to need a Savior are the ones who are most clearly in need of one. Without Christ who would deliver them from the power of death, they turn the silliest things into a god.

216

All things are possible in Christ

Were the strength of Christ not manifest in our life, those who hate us would not be so intently doing all they can to provoke us to fall from grace. This is just another blessing for which we must give God thanks continually—he gives us the strength necessary to resist lowering ourselves to our enemies' level.

217

Ruusbroec again

The love of God of which Jan van Ruusbroec spoke many centuries ago is just as available to us today as it was to him. The way we periodize history—ancient, medieval, modern, or whatever—is not wholly without basis. Still, in the end, a human being is a human being no matter the time and circumstances in which he finds himself. The choice is always the same—to be of the world or to be of God.

218

Marion's "saturated phenomenon" was for me a gift

In response to the long tradition of Christian mystics who have had so much to say about God on the basis of their religious experience, Kant contends that God in fact cannot be the object of any possible experience. Hence, his criticism of what he terms "enthusiasm." We owe it to Marion to have demonstrated that the Kantian account of experience, which equates the conditions of possible experience with those of objects, does not foreclose the possibility of God's appearing. God, who is not revealed as an object, is encountered as a "saturated" phenomenon. When I read this response to Kant many years ago, it struck me as correct, and I remain just as convinced now of its truth as I did at the time.

219

Surpassing Merleau-Ponty

It is a commonplace to read that Merleau-Ponty breaks with so much of philosophical tradition (here the arch-villain is Descartes, or at least, "Cartesianism"), by emphasizing the centrality of the body to being-in-the-world. But Merleau-Ponty's account of the body is fundamentally misleading. He treats the body as an opening onto the world alone, as if it were not also available to God.

220

Ontological monism

Among today's phenomenologists, Emmanuel Falque sees this better than most. However, his attempt to distance himself from Henry prevents him from recognizing that it was Henry who in fact has provided the best demonstration of what is lacking in Merleau-Ponty's account of embodiment. "Ontological monism," Henry's term for the philosophical tradition's error of focusing only on transcendence, overlooks the interiority of embodiment—the dimension that doesn't open us to the world, but responds to the Spirit of God.

221

Jacobi

One remarkable illustration of today's nihilism is the fact that the individual responsible for coining the term, Friedrich Jacobi, is totally unknown.

222

Jacobi (cont'd)

Or rather, I should say that his name is not known widely. Nevertheless, his thought lives on in those whose thought it has influenced and those, in turn, who read those it has influenced. To wit, somewhere in *On the Divine Things and Their Revelation*, he remarks that all beings, including us, above all, *receive* our existence, that we are brought to life from beyond ourselves, and that not for a single moment do we hold our own living existence within our own power. As he then goes on to explain, in this respect, we are *breathing* creatures, which is to say, our preservation is in need of a constant flow from outside. Now, anyone familiar with the phenomenological tradition will recognize in this first idea the central guiding thought of Henry—we are living only insofar as we are always already the recipients of Life. And the second thought, namely the suggestion that such dependence can be likened to breath, is a principal one in Chrétien. Henry read very little of the history of philosophy, preferring instead to reach his own philosophical conclusions based on whatever his own phenomenological investigations brought into view (in this way, he was like Husserl.) Chrétien, for his part, read more than normal mortals could in a thousand lifetimes (and, in this way, he was more like Heidegger.) While it is thus very probable that Chrétien at some point encountered this passage in Jacobi, whereas Henry never did, the question of influence is neither here nor there. For here it is more fundamentally a matter of inspiration: the same thought, expressed first by Jacobi, then later by Henry and Chrétien, is in each instance an expression of originality, for it is not a truth originating from having read a page in this or that text, but rather an encounter with what has itself called forth its articulation—the Breath of Life.

223

The crisis of meaning

The historicity of sense—this means meaning is historical. As Husserl observes, this entails that meaning is fragile—it can disappear if it is not preserved, sustained, and transmitted. According to Husserl, our contemporary crisis of meaning, one he characterizes as a crisis of reason, is rooted in scientism—all truthfulness is now thought according to the methods and results appropriate to the natural and mathematical sciences. This in turn begets a forgetfulness of the lifeworld and the transcendental subjectivity that is at the source of such meaning. For Husserl, the one responsible for all this is Galileo. Then Heidegger comes along, telling a different story about the origin of nihilism. For Heidegger, the oblivion of being, the forgetfulness of being, is so complete that "only a god can save us." Henry, however, is the one to have thought the phenomenological critique of nihilism to its completion. Galilean objectivism and naturalism do lead to a forgetfulness of subjectivity. But what Henry insists on, correctly, is that forgetfulness of subjectivity is ultimately a forgetfulness of God. Hence, Henry will claim that only Christ can save us, for in him alone is Life.

224

Nihilism (cont'd)

Our culture's descent into nihilism is not therefore rooted in scientism (Husserl) or even the forgetting of being (Heidegger). Its malaise of meaninglessness is the result of forgetting Christ, the one by whom and for whom all things were created, in which all things consist.

225

Twice removed from God

Aristotle made much of the fact that we naturally delight in perceiving the world's surroundings. In one of his texts (I believe it is the *History of the Concept of Time*), Heidegger remarks on this fact, characterizing this kind of perceptual "absorption" in our environment as a form of inauthenticity. Today, nearly a hundred years on, it is easy to see why Heidegger eventually came to conclude that technology is the underlying culprit for exacerbating inauthenticity. Long gone is a time when just being absorbed in perceiving the world around us could distract us from God. Now it is far worse, for, distracted by screens, we don't even find ourselves pulled into absorption in the world. Where before one had to overcome the temptation to absorb oneself in the world in order instead to ascend to God, now one must first overcome the temptation to stay engrossed in screens to first reenter one's environment. It is easy to see that there is something demonic about technology, for it seems to be designed to divert us from focusing on God.

226

The spirit of technology

The demonic origins of technology are recounted in Enoch, though I've never read the text carefully. What Enoch says, it seems to me, has been borne out by what we can all see for ourselves today.

227

The promise of immortality

Some of those who take the "death of God" as settled fact have attempted to console themselves by imagining that leaving a legacy can be an adequate substitute for personal immortality. One will live on posthumously, so they say, through the memory of those who continue to appreciate one's life and work—this is Voltaire, etc. Today's transhumanists are right to reject the Enlightenment's conception of immortality. It is inadequate to man's desires. Man does not want to be remembered after he has died; he wants to live forever. At bottom, however, both the Enlightener and the transhumanist peddle myths. The promise of immortality resides in Jesus Christ alone.

228

Chrétien's testament

For example, Chrétien, who undoubtedly continues to live on through his words, does so precisely insofar as his words were the expression of his life's commitment to the Word. We can admire Chrétien easily, not only because of what he wrote, but because we can honestly picture the man himself now in heaven.

229

Kierkegaard vs Heidegger

To return to the matter of conscience: Heidegger is incorrect when he asserts that the call of conscience comes from an anonymous caller. We can hear the Word of God echoing within us so long as we are willing. "Oh, but that is just Kierkegaard, and Heidegger rejects Kierkegaard," you will say. Indeed! Heidegger goes to considerable lengths in *Being and Time* to differentiate his existential analytic from Kierkegaard. But the influence is too unmistakable, which is why Husserl himself could tell Shestov that in order to understand what Heidegger was up to, one must first read Kierkegaard. I will only add that after one has read Kierkegaard and then read Heidegger, it seems clear to me that Kierkegaard is the one who emerges as correct.

230

Two arguments for "methodological" atheism

What damage to truth can be done in the name of fealty to philosophical method! In one breath, one attempts to justify methodological atheism in the name of the phenomenological reduction. In the next breath, one attempts to justify it also by appeal to the Husserlian standard of *Evidenz*—God is not given clearly and distinctly, etc., etc. But what the reduction itself is, and in what performing it correctly precisely consists, is not at all a clear and distinct matter. To the contrary, the nature and purpose of the reduction has been a point of contention since phenomenology's inception. We now face an obvious contradiction. The initial appeal to the reduction as a justification for methodological atheism has itself run afoul of the epistemic standard of *Evidenz* that was alleged to rule out the appearing of God. That these two main reasons cited to justify the bracketing of God from phenomenology cancel each other out—what else may we conclude but that there is nothing truly *methodological* about such atheism? "Reduction," "Evidenz," etc.—when those who oppose the "theological turn" of phenomenology deploy this arsenal of methodological terminology, it's just an ad hoc explanation meant to justify the original desire to ignore God.

231

Two arguments for "methodological" atheism (cont'd)

What I think, in short, is that those who most vehemently oppose the "theological turn" are not just atheists, strictly speaking. It is not so much that they disbelieve there is a God as it is that they hate God. Thomas Nagel, a famous antitheist, states quite openly that he wants atheism to be true, that he hopes there is no God, that it would be bad if God were to exist. The worst of all possible worlds is one in which there is a God—that's the main idea. This is why those who try to bracket God from phenomenology have so much to say about how phenomenology's task is to attend to the world apart from God—in this way, they can imagine a world in which they get what they want, in short, one where there is no God. The practice of phenomenology as methodological atheism becomes an ascetic escape from their being before God.

232

On a bench in Cambria

Camus, Sartre, Heidegger—so many of the influential twentieth-century philosophers speak almost exclusively of the "negative": boredom, anxiety, absurdity, grief, betrayal, and, of course, nothingness itself. Years ago, my father remarked on this and asked me what "rule" would forbid someone from formulating a philosophy of existence that privileged the "positive": love, joy, gratitude, and so forth. (I recently encountered a passage in which Kevin Hart remarks on the same fact.) The truth is that the decision to prioritize the moods and attitudes and phenomena the atheistic existentialists did is just that, a *decision*. We're free not to follow their example.

233

Henry the great unmasker

I have noticed a particularly strong aversion to Michel Henry among those who dislike the "theological turn." I think the antipathy those feel toward him is due largely to the fact that they detect a certain Pelagianism in his outlook concerning the relation between God and man—that we are naturally able to obey God, that God is always already revealed to us, and that it is we who must decide how to respond to God's call. Those, then, who ordinarily can plead ignorance to knowledge of God resent that Henry unmasks them—as Henry notes, there is no way to be truly ignorant of God, for Christ, who is Life, has brought us into our condition of living.

234

"The death of the death of God"

By the end of this century, everyone will talk of the "death of the death of God" (the expression is Marion's). No longer anymore will it be simply assumed, as it was in the twentieth century, that Nietzsche and other atheists had pronounced the last word on God. When the spell of atheism is at last dispelled, then the problem will be what it was before: in Christendom everyone thinks he is a Christian, even when he isn't. Still, this is a state of affairs far preferable to what we have now, one that puts Sodom and Gomorrah to shame. These things take considerable time before they come to pass, even if it is obvious to those with eyes to see that they will.

235

In the Ryle Room

I wrote earlier, in reference to Heidegger, of the "vanity of authenticity." Marion highlights the experience of vanity with an eye to formulating what he terms the "erotic reduction." His claim is simple: that only God's love makes life worth living, for everything else is subject, in our darkest moments, to the question: "What's the use?" Even the practice of phenomenological philosophy itself, as understood by Husserl and Heidegger, is ultimately vain, insofar as it is subject to vanity's question. For what's really the use in describing the universal structures of the world, or of explicating the structures of Dasein's existence, or attempting to formulate the question of the meaning of Being, if, in the end, we truly were thrown into a world that had come from nowhere, and was headed nowhere, and for no reason at all? Were that the case, the desire to describe the world would be a kind of pathology, a sort of vain amusement that ultimately served no end other than to ward off boredom and anxiety, until, of course, the dark hour of vanity visited us, and we realized that we had been kidding ourselves the whole time. But when we recognize God, whatever we go on to do in philosophy reflects God's love. The phenomenological task of description is no longer vain, for it has passed into praise.

236

Kafka

Must we all be Joseph K, consigned to the ordeal of absurdity? We read literature, in part, to make sense of life. What happens, then, when we read a novel such as *The Trial*, which, in attempting to make sense of life, comes to the conclusion that the effort is futile, for there is no such meaning? In order to find meaning in the face of life's apparent absurdity, we must think with Kafka against Kafka.

237

Christ is the door

At the parable's conclusion, the doorkeeper tells K, "No one else could ever be admitted here, since this gate was made only for you. I am now going to shut it." Whether it was intentional or not on Kafka's part, one's mind turns immediately to the biblical description of the kingdom of heaven's being taken by force. K never gains entry to the law because he fails to take it by force. Christ is the Door, yet we must choose to enter in.

238

Coram Deo

For my own part, when doing philosophy, thinking on anything else but God and our relation to him has seemed ancillary. For when I got to thinking about the meaning of being before God, there was always more to think, the importance of which is beyond compare.

239

My Berlin

I think that a true repetition is impossible. As Kierkegaard learned through his return trip to Berlin, no two experiences are identical. And yet, at the same time, we do nevertheless justifiably say of another day when asked how it went, "Oh, nothing happened," "Same old, same old," or "You know, the usual." No two experiences are precisely identical, but so much of everyday life is banal. This paradox—that daily life is at once the same yet also mysteriously singular—is just another way that God tries to reach us, reminding us that there is more than meets the eye to mundane existence.

240

The form of the scoundrel according to Lewis

Although it is a piece not mentioned nearly as often as his other essays and novels, I believe "The Inner Ring" is C. S. Lewis's finest account of the world's illusions. The best evidence that Lewis has hit the mark in what he says there is that the piece is conspicuously ignored. People don't like to give it the credit it deserves, because it stings—they see themselves in what Lewis condemns.

241

The honor that comes from God only

The world can name a street in your honor, erect a statue of you in the square, commemorate your life with a yearly festival, etc., etc., etc. Yet what good is all that honor from men if one was cast away by God? All the hidden lives of those who lived humbly before God matter infinitely more than do the lives of Napoleon, Einstein, or whomever the history books vaunt. The great man is the one who humbles himself before God. Everything else is vanity.

242

Dreaming spires

The snow falling on the Deer Park is indescribably beautiful, majestic even. But being able to enjoy the view on a daily basis would not have been worth the price of selling my soul. So I will visit when I can, and that is good enough.

243

"Like a movie"

Said to me on a park bench in Oxford: "It's like living in *The Firm*." Indeed! That is why, as I said in response to my friend, it is pointless to seek a vindication for all the wrong that had been done to him. The truth is that those who hate us will never accept that we had always been right. And those who love us already know that we are. The only vindication that matters, even in this life, is the one that comes from God. Forget what others think.

244

"Devastating, Mitch"

Someone in Oxford who, at the time, I had believed was a friend of mine once pointed out to me that every man can be understood, to a large extent, in light of his relation to a combination of three temptations: women, money, and power. As this son of a famous Bollywood director explained it, a man strongly desires the one, would prefer to go with rather than without the second, and is finally largely indifferent to the third. He said this expecting me to divulge my profile. Years later, his comment made sense, when I had realized that the world runs on blackmail, bribery, and threats. If we live lives of holy self-control, however, evil no longer has any dominion over us, for we have nothing to hide, we are not greedy or covetous, and we have no fear of death.

245

They are of Cain

Two road accidents (the first of which killed its target, the second of which put its victim in a coma), three physical assaults (the last of which prompted the police officers at the scene to contact homicide detectives to determine who was possibly paying to have me killed), tampering with my car tires, a break-in, etc., etc., etc.—so you see, when this friend in Oxford spoke to me of *The Firm*, he knew I am someone, given what I have experienced too, who would understand what he means. To be sure, Christians today are no longer thrown to the lions in a spectacle for public entertainment, but I can think of no other explanation for the incredible series of events I have undergone over the last ten years besides that those who have done what they have done (and still gotten away with it!) did so because their hatred of Christ is so great that they will stop at nothing to hound those who directly oppose their evil.

246

Paris 2018

There are a certain few who early on identified my work for what it is and made clear to me that they were supporting it because they knew I was the one to whom they would pass the baton. I will run my leg of the race, writing what I can, till it is time to hand over the baton to whomever comes along next to take over.

247

In patience

It has been ten years of incredible tribulation, and I now see the wisdom behind the patience of Job. My persecutors have tried to strip me of everything, but have failed. Not only does the work continue, but I already have all that I need—the hope of glory in Christ Jesus.

248

!

A note arrived yesterday much to my surprise, both because of the sender and its message. It contained no explicit comment on the past, and so, in that respect, it was not an apology. (This is fine, I've always tried to be someone who doesn't need apologies.) But the fact that the sender wrote at all (and without hostility!) was without doubt an act of acknowledgment—well, of so much that has still never been said. If anyone reads these aphorisms and feels that they were somehow targeted against him, know they were not written in malice. I wrote them because I have felt called, and besides, there is so much more I could have written than I have or probably ever will.

249

The power of devotion

I must allow myself one further thought on yesterday's extraordinary development. Perhaps it is self-serving of me to conclude so, but when he read the manuscript, did the reader not see that, even if I am wrong, it would be good if I were to be correct? In other words, even if he himself still does not yet have faith in Christ—if in that respect he is still blind—has he not yet at least seen how desperate life would be without the promise of eternal life in Christ? One gets old, retires, and sees that all of the world's lures were just that—diversions. This alone would be incredible progress—to move from supposed indifference, or even antipathy, toward God to a recognition that it would be good if faith is justified, is true. That is truly something! God is always wiling to meet us where we are, so long as we will turn to meet him.

250

Peacemakers

I'm now put in mind of a verse that has always been a source of hope for me. "When a man's ways please the Lord, he maketh even his enemies to be at peace with him"—true! I would never dare to suggest I can alter what Scripture has said for the sake of the truth, for Scripture is the breath of God, but with that essential qualification in mind, I should add simply that when an enemy makes peace with us, there is a sense in which he discovers that we were never really enemies to begin with. Someone might argue that whether one is an enemy or not is an asymmetrical affair—it is sufficient for someone to be an enemy if he simply counts himself as being one, irrespectively of how we feel ourselves towards him (the same goes in reverse, of course: someone can in a sense be my enemy, regardless of how he feels towards me, if I view him as one). In any case, when an enemy makes peace with us precisely because our ways have pleased the Lord, he sees that he merely *thought* we had been his enemy—for if our ways have truly pleased the Lord, we have always wished for the good of even those who saw themselves as our enemies.

251

Where your treasure lies

I know it's the *love* of money that is said to be the root of all evil, not money itself. Even if one doesn't love it, however, there is always something filthy and unseemly about money matters.

252

Rich in faith

What I write makes no money. If I were to write for money, what made the money would not be worth having written apart from that. How is a writer to live?

253

There is no freedom apart from peace

People today want "success"; if they are more abstractly minded, they will say it's "freedom" that interests them. What they should really seek is peace, the gift of which is found in Jesus Christ alone.

254

Brother heron

I made it to the sea, after all. Nothing has changed about it, and I find that a great comfort. Oh, let me be as steadfast as the sea!

255

Expectations

I came to the sea eager to write something sad, something bittersweet. At the shore, a ripping wind blew over the dunes, a whistling shrill cry of winter's desolation. And yet, standing there beneath thick fog that veiled the frothing waves from clear sky high above and out of sight, I discovered within me, to my surprise, not the forecasted grey of melancholy, but rather only unanticipated joy. Oh, Lord, how frail we are, that even our own moods surprise and astonish us! All I know is that I love you, and that it is because of you that life is not a dark saying.

256

Nature's half-spoken words

The gulls were far lovelier than I had imagined. They huddled together, braving the cold water, the bitter wind, everything about the desolate beach that explained why there was not another person in sight for miles. They did not speak, yet their silence was instructive, for it was a muteness that nevertheless taught me something. It will sound contradictory, but I don't think a man can begin to understand his infinite worth in the eyes of God until he has felt his utter insignificance in the eyes of the birds and nature's other creatures.

257

Samuel

One might call this text a notebook—that is what it has in effect become, anyway. I have written for myself, more or less unconcerned with attempting to persuade others of the truth of what I have to say by deductive argument. That is not because what I say is irrational, nor because I have resorted to mere assertion—rather, it is because I don't believe it is possible for such truths to be appreciated but by intuition, by seeing for oneself. I can attempt to induce others to see what I see, if it is indeed there to be seen, yet I cannot *force* anyone to do so. This, as it happens, is why most of what passes for "rational" philosophical dispute is really a waste of time: in the final analysis, people believe what they *want* to believe, regardless of what any argument suggests (and, in any case, any argument always rests on convictions, assumptions, beliefs, "intuitions" is what professional analytic philosophers call them, which ultimately must be presupposed in the argument itself). That being said, I do feel called here to address an objection that will have arisen in the mind of my imagined reader. There are in fact two objections that are related. First, have I not overstated the isolation of faith? For is there not the "communion of saints," "fellowship," etc., etc.? Yes, certainly. And that matters! Yet fellowship and community presuppose sincere commitment on the part of the individuals who comprise it, and the origin of that individual commitment can never be explained as a consequence of the community itself. One *enters* into the community, and only then can any fellowship be said in turn to help sustain that act of faith, that commitment, of each of those who so enters. (And even then, as helpful as others are, faith is only as strong as the one who possesses it; this is why, after all, there are those who depart from the faith; doing so is ultimately a personal choice.) Second, have I not been too harsh, too judgmental, confrontational even, when it comes to atheists and the world at large? I acknowledge that my rhetoric may at times be sharp. Still, I must insist that, regardless of the impression it may make to the contrary, I truly am writing from a place of sincere gentleness. So, for instance, when I say that we are in a way fundamentally alone in this life, I say so not out of cynicism, or egoism, or callousness, or pride, but only because I myself have many times experienced the incredible depths of a heartfelt encounter made possible with others and yet recognize that, despite these sacred moments of connection, there is a loneliness to existence, one that is all the more apparent in light of these profound, yet fleeting, moments of connection. For example, recently I was standing in my front yard, smoking a cigarette on a cold afternoon. A homeless man walked by, stopped at the gate, and asked for one. I gave him one, invited him to the porch to sit down, and then asked whether he would like some food. He told me his story—he was alone, having walked all the way across town to what was his encampment nearby. I was the only person to acknowledge him on his journey, much less offer to help, he said. When he left with some things I'd given him—and it wasn't much, because we hadn't gone grocery shopping in a while—he walked along for a bit, then turned back to me a few houses down, smiled, and said, "You are a good person." I routinely have these kinds of encounters. I do not relate this particular anecdote to boast of my good deeds or to use it as fodder for an argument. I recount it because, from what I have seen, we are indeed, in a certain regard, alone—the most downtrodden, desperate people I meet tell me this, tell me that nearly everyone else they have come across that day before receiving my help has ignored them. And even when we do pause to help, unlike most others who don't do so, we cannot deliver the other from his plight completely or permanently. At most, we can momentarily alleviate his suffering and sorrow. Only God can sustain the other through his life's ordeals. If someone reading this says, "Fair enough, but this one anecdote about his being helpful and concerned with another in need doesn't change the fact that he still sounds harsh and judgmental in his writing, which then makes me wonder just how sincere his supposed acts of kindness really are." I can only state that, if you are such a reader, now you are in effect judging me. That is entirely fine; you are free to form an opinion of the author. I do not wish to exempt myself from criticism, much less suggest that I am the only good Samaritan in the world. Far from it. But I have done what I can to help others in need often enough to know just how rare such a gesture is. In my experience, at least, it is because there are so few who help others that the world rightly deserves scorn for being the cruel and selfish place it is. There are atheists who can read my critical remarks about the world and claim that I am being unfair to others. And yet, many of these very same individuals would themselves have walked right by the homeless man whom I've mentioned, without paying him so much as a thought. Although the performative contradiction is glaring, it is hardly surprising: why would we expect them to recognize and hate the world for its cruelty and hypocrisy when they are at home in it?

258

Alone before God

In everyday life, in short, we no doubt exist alongside others, in that no question as to whether others besides myself exist can seriously arise—the Cartesian problem of other minds is foolishness. Nonetheless, there is another sort of solipsism at work in everyday life, an ethical one, one rooted in transcendental egoism. When we break free of this egoism and die to self, we become responsive and receptive to others in a fashion we hadn't previously. There follow all sorts of wonderful encounters of solidarity, of compassion, of kindness, of empathy, very often with similarly attuned strangers. But even then, when we respond to someone in compassion, or someone responds to us with compassion, we ultimately find that we are alone before God, at least most of the time. For the kind, compassionate other enters and departs our experience like an angel, delivering his or her message, and then we once again are left surrounded by others who, lost in the preoccupations of daily life's busyness, do not even see us. One is just another faceless face in the crowd.

259

Not even a sparrow

Yes, how monstrous it would be if there were no God in heaven who were watching us all, concerned with each and every one of us among the throng of innumerable people, always concerned with us, even if, to the world, it is as if we don't exist. There is such a God in heaven, and when we notice the other and respond to him with the attention for which the situation calls, we spread some of God's love in a loveless world. We can remind another that if an insignificant stranger such as ourselves cares about him, surely God in heaven does.

260

The tranquil madness of partial hopelessness

Were we to abandon the illusion that the future of society, or historical progress, or some political development, or collective human *telos* stands to change the fact that we must confront death ourselves, yet without hope in God or immortality, we would be bound to slip into madness. Camus, for one, certainly wondered whether that was the case. People today, however, are far too breezy in their nihilism, claiming as they do to be perfectly reconciled to their own future supposed annihilation and the annihilation of everyone they have known and loved in life. I believe that they don't fully understand what it is they say they believe. They're deluded. For if one contemplates the horrors and evils and injustices of this world, and then adds to that the further thought that death is simply the end of everything, that there is no future life in which this one will be justified, I don't see how to avoid drawing the conclusion that anyone who claims to believe this all, and believes it so casually, doesn't *really* believe it. What I'm getting at is that those who reject Christ haven't yet admitted how hopeless things would be if it were not for him and the promise of eternal life. When they say that they *do* admit and accept how hopeless things are, but that they find meaningful enjoyment in life nevertheless, here, again, it must be noted that they are self-deceived, for although they in effect *claim* to have abandoned all hope, they must still have *some* hope, however illusory, for they have not yet gone mad! This is the spiritual danger of our day's elevating the political to the religious. People do not even feel their personal need for Christ because they cling to the abstraction of a false political hope instead.

261

My friend Felipe

Proverbs declares that, in life, there is a friend who sticks closer to us than a brother. True! I am blessed to have many dear friends. Yet one, in particular, has always said plainly what he knew my enemies had at the time wanted me not to believe, wanted me to doubt—namely, that my work mattered, that it was worth pursuing, that it was touching those who did read it. He said so a number of years ago, before others ever would, and he said it purely because he recognized in it the same love of Christ he himself had and that he would have liked to express. Rather than becoming envious that he was not the one to have done the writing, he was simply grateful that I had said it for him. What a rare, generous spirit—one that rejoices in the truth. And this is why he has been attacked considerably in his own life. Yes, he has endured his own share of suffering, his own persecution, facing his trials with true humility and unusual steadfastness. That he has always admired my work for being an honest reflection of my life itself has motivated me to try to continue to live up to that judgment—if my work proves inspiring to readers like him, it is only because I try to speak from a place of genuine testimony of God's love, of all the wonderful things God has done for me. Over the years, through writing the books I have, and having him in turn read them, he and I have grown together in Christ. When he reads this entry, which I know will come as a surprise to him, I want him to know that God loves him for everything he has done in faithfulness to the truth, no matter whether those in his daily life fail to recognize and appreciate it.

262

Barnacle

I almost tore myself away from this page, feeling daunted by the inadequacy that comes with trying to put into words what you mean to me, what your love has done for me. No matter what I say, I know it will not be good enough. Yet I shall write something, anyway. I believe that you need me, and I don't say so in a spirit of possessiveness. I say it with gratitude, that someone needs me—I think that to go a lifetime without feeling needed, without feeling loved, would be the most hideous of hells, and you've delivered me from that. If I may say so, I think what we have is special, and I say it knowing it's a cliché, but even if many others would say the same of their love, I must still insist they are mistaken and that they don't understand what we have. If I may be allowed to make a comparison, I don't think for a second that a love other than ours could have survived the ordeals we have (not from any conflict between us, but from external circumstances that have tested us). I've seen marriages buckle and collapse under the stress of much, much less. Those who need to know the details of what I mean already know. But I can say something about it here in general terms. Because there are similarities between my life and Kierkegaard's—to wit, I have powerful enemies among the establishment (I'm the opposite of the "British philosopher king" whom JD Vance calls his "sherpa" and "mentor"); I was lampooned publicly in the newspaper like Kierkegaard was (there is a deeper parallel on this point: just as Meir Goldschmidt of the *Corsair* was the son of a Rothschild, so it was a powerful cabal of well-connected figures at the college who were behind the smears directed against me in the Oxford *Cherwell*); I am blacklisted, and yet I remain a prolific writer nevertheless—sometimes other scholars contact me to tell me that they envy my having written so much, and that they wish that they had taken the path they believe I have taken, which, in their estimation, is one that they think would have required them never to have married, to have, as one such individual, a husband and father of four, put it to me, "pulled a Kierkegaard and not have married Regine." This is always incredibly humorous to me because of course I myself *am* married! "Marry and you will regret it / Don't marry, and you will regret it / Either way, you will regret it." I have to say that I have married and *don't* regret it. I would marry you all over again without the slightest hesitation. The idea that it would have been necessary not to marry in order to do the work I have done is pure nonsense—people who think that is true of themselves are fantasizing about something of which they know nothing. My only regret, really, if there is one, is that you have been made to suffer as a consequence of what has been done to us. If I had known what those who hate me would do in retribution for my defiance of them, I would have hesitated to marry you and warned you off against marrying me. But I know you wouldn't have listened, and that is why I love you. Really, as trying as things sometimes have been, they are not so bad at all. My only regret, frankly, is not the hardships that we have had to overcome together. No, my regret is that I still haven't fully accepted that our time together is so limited. I try to take solace in God's promise that, in the end, we shall be like the angels together, and this makes me feel vaguely better since, although our relationship will have been altered by eternity, it will never be over entirely. Far from romanticizing the notion of having given you up as a wife in the name of my work (as others have confessed to me that they secretly wish they had done for the sake of their own), I would gladly give up all my work if it were the price of being with you. Still, I know I have not yet addressed what you're after. You want to know *why* I love you. Why does the sun rise each morning and run its circuit over the earth? Why does the moon awaken each night to oversee the dark? Why do the tides flow? The seasons succeed one another in harmony? My love for you, really, is not all that different, for it was as natural and spontaneous as anything else governed by law. From the very moment I saw you, I knew you were meant for me, and I for you. I loved the intelligence in your eyes; the dimples in your smile; the way you closed your eyes when you would laugh; I loved your leather jacket; the way your hair brushed against your neck; the mole on your collarbone; but most of all, I loved that you understood that the world is one big stage, that nearly everyone is just pretending to be something he really isn't, and so, if there really is any true point to this life, it must lie in love alone.

263

One flesh

All that is to say, you are my best friend (no matter what Nick says).

264

Double rainbow

From my unassuming flat window, I beheld a double rainbow stretching over the shimmering Cathedral. Those walking along the rain-drenched street below, so eager to get inside to see what lies within the sandstone walls, hadn't the faintest idea of what truly lurked within the cloisters, things that, in any case, they'd never believe. Yes, things far, far stranger than anything even Hogwarts itself has to offer! At my window, I could not imagine them myself—though in time I came to experience them. All I knew was simply that I felt that I was alone and that, no matter where you are, no matter what you accomplish, you must come to terms with this fact—you are alone if you don't have God. Lord, thank you for not forsaking me there.

265

Beardo

Many years ago, at the college graduation party in California, my friend pointed to the world map hanging on his wall: "Each of you guys point to where you're going and what you're going to do." I pointed where I did, and I have gone on to do what I said I would. Only those who first believe in Providence will come to see it at work in their own lives.

266

Always seeking you

From here, to there, and from there to here again. Where have I truly been this whole time, but searching for you?

267

In God

Wherever you are—that is the place to be.

268

Horizons

That experience is horizonal means, among other things, that the past haunts a place's presence. Part of a place's present mood retains that of its history, and that history, while not merely being the sum of the individual histories of each of its objects, is nonetheless imbued by the inner horizons of each thing's career there. For instance, step inside an old café that one has not set foot inside for many years and you will see that, in a way, much about it has changed—the staff is different, as are the patrons. The former "regulars" have vanished, replaced by new ones. But are they truly gone completely? No—all the change rises up against the background of the traces of all those who are now present as absent, present in their absence. It is not that our memory imposes a "subjective" gloss over things. To the contrary, the past really is present in everything present. The carpet, the piano, the paintings, the tables, the chairs, the cups and the saucers, the mugs—all that once had been seen, heard, and handled by those who are no longer there in the flesh, but linger on, having left their mark, is now experienced by those today who themselves will in turn pass on, adding to the temporal thickness of the place.

269

Linnaea's

I think we were four—Brian, Matt, Shanan, and I. We'd been reading Alvin Plantinga and William Alston in our "Epistemology of Religious Belief" course. Brian invited me to join the reading group, to read something quite different—Kierkegaard's *Fear and Trembling*. I was an atheist then, and after the first reading, I knew I had the reaction they all hoped I would: "Well, what do you have to say to *that*?" Like Abraham, I was speechless. It took some years to work itself all out, but that text changed everything for me. The meet-up table by the window is across the room—looking at it, I can remember Brian removing his gloves and beanie that day with a smile on his face. *What does it mean?* We can't anticipate how our lives will touch those of others—I believe God's providence works through us in ways we could never foresee.

270

Numbness

Atheism is not unbelief in God; it is estrangement. In retrospect, I see that even when I considered myself an atheist, or an agnostic, God was always there. I think of that period in my life as being akin to the sleeper who awakens to find that he's slept on his arm wrong and it is now numb—he can't feel his arm as he ordinarily does, yet he knows it is there nonetheless. So it is with God. Sin numbs us, deadens us to God's presence. We can turn our back to him, but he is still there—waiting.

271

Linnaea's (cont'd)

You sat at the table reading Foucault right next to the one where I am now writing. I think it was evening. The place was crowded. I can't recall much else—I think I said hello, though I don't remember talking. Maybe I didn't intrude, in order not to interrupt the fact that you appeared to be immersed in the text. You were slightly younger then than I am now. On weekends, you made the drive north to visit the man in the green VW Karmann Ghia. He's dead now, and you long ago surprised everyone by getting where you did—such promise. And then—nothing. You told me all those years ago that if I weren't lazy, I might get into graduate school somewhere. I've tried to work hard. You used to work hard, too. What happened? I think you sold your soul when you got there.

272

Dawn came

You came to visit me. What Maldiney calls the "blockage" of melancholy had choked me up. Every hour was an eternity—pure agony. I had come as close as it is possible for someone to live while internalizing the belief that nothing truly mattered. Outside, on the patio, beneath the ivy and near the fountain, you told me: "It's always darkest before the dawn." I'm glad to have passed beyond that darkness. When the sun rose and the dawn arrived, it was a glimmer of the great Light that lights everyone who comes into the world. To walk in this Light, the true Light, one must be willing to leave behind the dark place. It took me far too long to accept that, to take responsibility for my existential posture (despair or joy)—but I did, and in no small part because of what you said. I choose to let my joy be full in the Light.

273

Vanity's question

"What's the use?" I now know. The point is to find and follow Christ Jesus.

274

Linnaea's (cont'd)

Books for me have always been an integral part of life. Still, life must be lived "off the page." An existential philosophy must never forget this, especially a Christian existentialism. Years ago, I read books here that touched me. Now I'm finishing a book that I hope will touch someone also. Nobody here at the café knows who I am—my works are unknown to them. Some of the college's philosophy students have perhaps heard my name—they certainly know at least about phenomenology. When you read this, whoever you are, and you wonder what to do with yourself, with your life, understand that God's claim, which is apparent on my work, a claim that has led me full-circle from philosophy student to writer in this café, is the same claim that he has on you. So, by all means read, read, read. No matter how extensively you read in life about life, never forget that what matters ultimately is *life itself*, that your name, when your life is over, should be counted worthy of being listed in the Book of Life.

275

Your path

Yet what *exactly* are you to do? Where *precisely* are you to go? Nobody has the right answers to these questions but you yourself—they must come from what God will put on your heart (if you listen). If you do this, if you listen, you will be on the narrow way that leads to eternal life. Few there be who find it. Most everyone passes through life thinking he is the captain of his ship, at the helm, plotting a course through the world, always with some destination, some goal, some port, as it were, in view. But it is all a mirage. Spiritually understood, such lives are directionless and aimless. You must be different. Let God chart your path rather than plotting your own. Follow him, and you will not regret it.

276

Redeeming the time

Following Christ, it should be emphasized, almost always doesn't involve anything that the world considers adventurous, remarkable, or momentous. It will in all likelihood be a very quiet, obscure life that you lead. Rather than looking out at the world with an eye of ambition and dreaming of success, work instead on purifying yourself within, freeing yourself of sin, and growing in virtue. What you achieve through this life in the Spirit will be far more extraordinary than the achievements of those the world considers great but who die without Christ, lost in their sins.

277

We are not nothing

Camus was right, and Sartre was wrong: there is a human nature. I would go so far as to say that each and every individual has a unique essence, if you like, what makes him uniquely and distinctly himself. (This unique essence counts as a universal human nature because it reflects, in its own way, the *imago Dei* in which we are all made.) There are things about us (personality traits, dispositions, sensibilities, mannerisms, interests, talents, aptitudes, habits, etc.) without which we would not be who we are. At the same time, we are free. Free, ultimately, either to answer or refuse our calling from God. For it is up to us to cultivate and shape our personalities. Despair, as Kierkegaard understood it, is the failure to do so, the failure (he would say refusal) to shape ourselves in accord with what God intends, given the way he has fashioned us as the unique person we are. In kindergarten, for example, everyone in my class did an assignment in which each of us was asked to list everything we liked to do. "Swimming and reading, nothing else," I said. All these years later, not much has changed! That the man I am today can recognize himself in the child he was then leads me to believe that I am on the right path. I'm not a stranger to myself, which is to say, through God, I'm learning to be myself.

278

Limits

Karl Jaspers states that it is impossible for us to grasp the totality, for we live in the midst of it. Nonetheless, we do have an *experience* of totality, of wholeness, of beings as a whole, even if that reality exceeds what we can grasp conceptually. A grasp of totality of the sort systematic metaphysics seeks eludes us. The same may even be said of our own individual life. Can we ever grasp the whole of it, understand it as a totality, while we live in the midst of it? And, of course, there is so much about the heavens and earth that must remain unknown to us. Even other persons are a mystery. These limits to our understanding should constrain our thirst for clarity and intelligibility. Life demands learning to live without certitudes. For although absolute intellectual clarity escapes us, there is sufficient clarity of purpose in humbly doing the will of God.

279

After metaphysics

I now have already spent half a lifetime trying to make sense of the very urge itself to make sense of life. Along the way, the yearning to make sense of everything involved the longing to make sense of those who are, or have been, dearest to me. Alas, ever elusive, they passed through, veiled in mystery. Life, I thus can now see, does not admit of the kind of sense I for so long had thought it would eventually. For if we cannot ever fully make sense of the others whom we know so well that we, in a certain regard, do know them better than they even know themselves, what hope is there for thinking we might somehow bring the whole of existence into systematic view? The idea is preposterous. Yet this metaphysical urge for clarity is not so much an aspiration that strikes me as hubristic, arrogant, or foolish—though it is that. More basically, it is confused; a category mistake; something in a way that is itself senseless. Anyone who comes to understand life recognizes it is not a problem to be solved by the sciences or even philosophy, but rather a mystery to be navigated by faith.

280

Lord, help my unbelief

"If you have faith, you would move a mountain." This is not figurative or the least hyperbolic. No, the Lord meant it quite seriously, and I believe it. Or rather, I believe that he meant sincerely that if I had such faith, I could indeed command a mountain to move and that it would. Sometimes I have thought about turning to the wilderness and spending the rest of my life attempting to command the mountain to move. I'm defeated before I ever begin, which is why I will never attempt to begin measuring up to this particular test of faithfulness. For when I think about it, I realize that I would lose heart, that I will never truly attempt such a thing. For me, the idea remains only that—an idea. How humbling to recognize that our faith, however strong it may be, can always grow stronger, that is to say, is never yet as strong as it could be. Lord, help me with my unbelief.

281

Husserl's error

Let's revisit this idea of infinity, the evidence of God. We all know what Descartes had to say on the subject, which is why he first of all came to mind at the outset of these fragments. But what of Husserl? For Husserl, the God of transcendental phenomenology is a value, an idea, not a person. The closest his phenomenology comes to the God of Christianity is when it acknowledges the ethical imperative of loving one's neighbor. But even here, this is a rational idea grounded in the teleology of transcendental life—not a living command animating our heart through the power of the Holy Ghost. I have no doubt that Husserl was a sincere Christian (many of his atheistic readers ignore that)—I simply wonder why he expended so much effort attempting to lay the philosophical foundation of universal humanity on anything else but the Rock of Christ.

282

Revelation

We don't begin with an idea of God. Revelation originates from God himself.

283

The Scriptures read us

The wiser we become, the more difficult it is for us to express life's truths. The trouble is not that they are too complicated to communicate, but rather that their simplicity is beyond words. That is why I always turn to the Proverbs and the Psalms in order to find the words I can't find. I find there articulated what could not have been said without divine inspiration. The Scriptures express the thoughts I can't. They read me.

284

Nightingale soul

One could go on writing indefinitely, for there is always more to say if one so chooses, but a work must come to an end somewhere. I feel like a bird who has sung its evening song—perhaps there will be another day tomorrow, and thus more to be sung, but for now I have said enough.

285

In a word

Just one more thought! Knowing God does not demand a science of God. Even an existentialist philosophy elucidating the experience of being before God is no substitute for being before him. Knowing the true and living God, what else is it really but a matter of obedience from the heart?

286
The last word

Lord be praised, that I may preach from my study.

Index of Names

Adorno, Theodor, 53
Alston, William, 105
Ammons, Archibald Randolph, 75
Aristotle, 84
Augustine, Saint, 105

Bonaparte, Napoleon, 90
Borges, Jorge Luis, 27

Camus, Albert, 3, 4, 30, 35, 74, 79, 87, 100, 109
Carroll, Lewis, 70
Chrétien, Jean-Louis ix, 11, 19, 82, 85
Claudel, Paul, 19

Dante Alighieri, 60
Demas, 79
Descartes, René, 1, 6, 9, 81, 111
Dostoevsky, Fyodor, 23, 59, 74

Einstein, Albert, 90
Enoch, 84
Esau, 36

Falque, Emmanuel, 81
Faulkner, William, 40, 41
Feuerbach, Ludwig, 24
Fichte, Johann Gottlieb, 56
Foucault, Michel, 106

Goethe, Johann Wolfgang von, 63

Hamann, Johann Georg, 22
Hart, Kevin, 87
Heidegger, Martin, 46, 51, 53, 64, 67, 71, 76, 82, 83, 84, 85, 87, 88
Henry, Michel ix, 75, 81, 82, 83, 87

Housset, Emmanuel, 62, 71
Hume, David, 49
Husserl, Edmund, 69, 71, 76, 82, 83, 85, 86, 88, 111

Jacobi, Friedrich Heinrich, 82
Janicaud, Dominique, 49
Jaspers, Karl, 110
John the Baptist, 60

Kafka, Franz, 89
Kandinsky, Wassily, 63
Kant, Immanuel, 6, 49, 63, 74, 81
Kierkegaard, Søren, 9, 24, 38, 54, 76, 85, 90, 102, 105, 109
King David, 34

Lacoste, Jean-Yves ix, 64
Lewis, Clive Staples, 90

Maldiney, Henri, 107
Marion, Jean-Luc ix, 77, 81, 88
Merleau-Ponty, Maurice, 81
Merton, Thomas, 20
Moore, George Edward, 66

Newton, Isaac, 63
Nietzsche, Friedrich, 25, 26, 36, 88

Paul, Saint, 10, 29, 34, 42, 55, 59, 69, 78
Pelagius, 69
Plantinga, Alvin, 105
Plato, 5, 6, 61, 71

Richard, St Victor of, 54
Ricœur, Paul, 9, 52, 64
Rilke, Rainer Maria, 59

Index of Names

Robinson, Marilynne, 19, 73
Rousseau, Jean-Jacques, 26
Russell, Bertrand, 66
Ruusbroec, John van, 53, 80

Sartre, Jean-Paul, 49, 52, 87, 109
Schopenhauer, Arthur, 47
Shestov, Lev, 73, 85
Spurgeon, Charles, 77

Tarkovsky, Andrei, 77
Tertullian, 30

Vance, James David, 102
Voltaire, 49, 85

Wittgenstein, Ludwig, 22

Žižek, Slavoj, 67

www.ingramcontent.com/pod-product-compliance
Lightning Source LLC
Chambersburg PA
CBHW031347160426
43196CB00007B/766